RED PANDA ACTIVITY

BOOK 1

ART ADVENTURES

SARA VETTETH

RED PANDA

Published by Red Panda, an imprint of Westland Books, a division of Nasadiya Technologies Private Limited, in 2025

No. 269/2B, First Floor, 'Irai Arul', Vimalraj Street, Nethaji Nagar, Alapakkam Main Road, Maduravoyal, Chennai 600095

Westland, the Westland logo, Red Panda and the Red Panda logo are the trademarks of Nasadiya Technologies Private Limited, or its affiliates.

ISBN: 9789371975773

10 9 8 7 6 5 4 3 2 1

Text by Sara Vetteth with Kavya Avula and Nivedha Leoni
Illustrated by Carolyn Susanna P. (all activity-based illustrations) and Anya Viji (Cat City and illustrations of artists)
Book design by Lubnaa Maryam
Book Design Consultant: Valentina Abenavoli

Printed at Thomson Press (India) Ltd

Table of Contents

Art supplies you will need

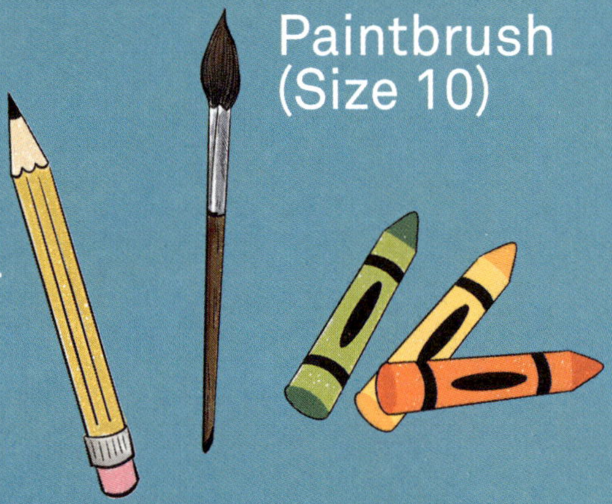

Pencil

Paintbrush (Size 10)

Oil pastels

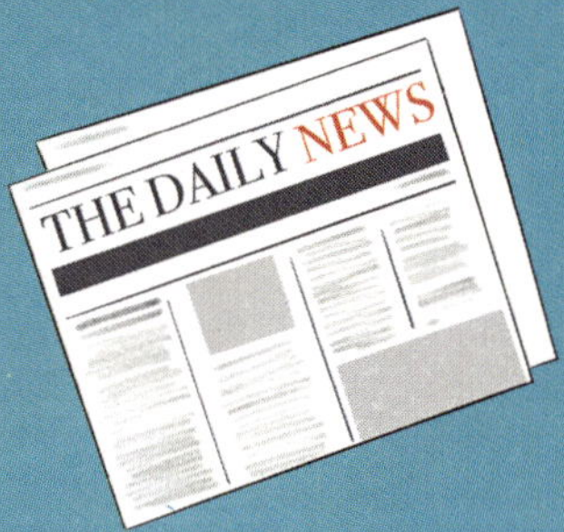

Newspaper

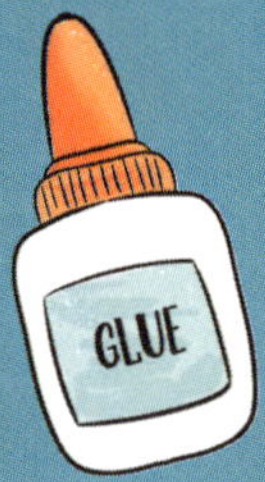

Glue

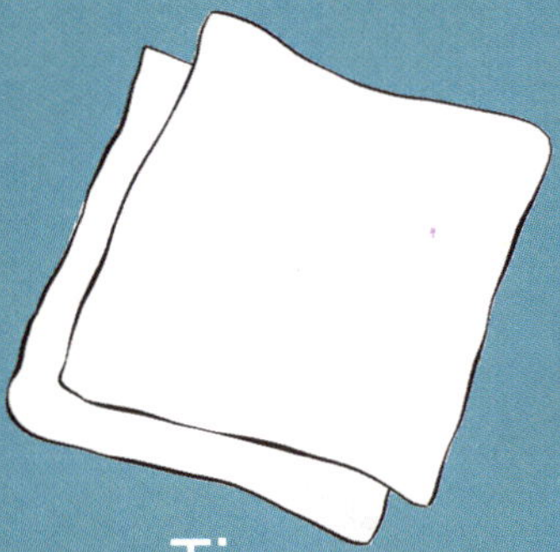

Tissue papers

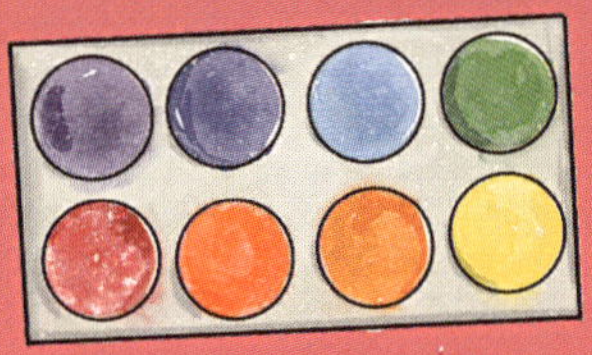

Watercolour paints

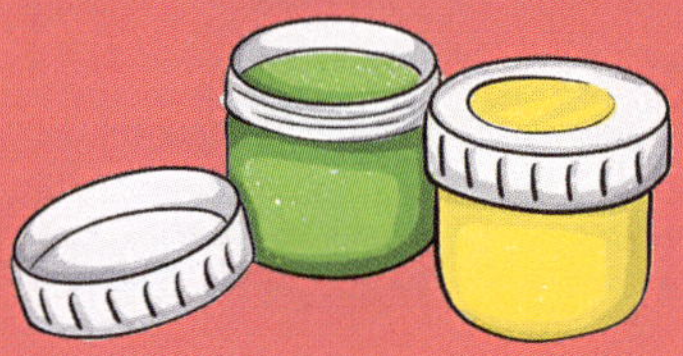

Poster paints / tempera paints

or

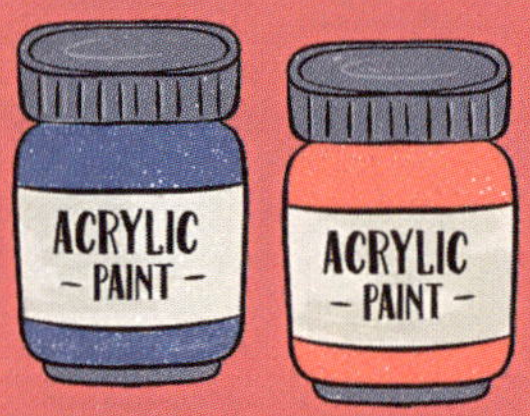

Acrylic paints

Many of our activities need paints.
You can use any of these.

This book

belongs to

_ _ _ _ _ _ _ _ _ _ _ _ _ _ _ _

Dots and Spots

We see dots all around us.
On the back of a ladybug,
the shape of seeds or
buttons on your shirt.
Look around you and
see if you can find more dots!

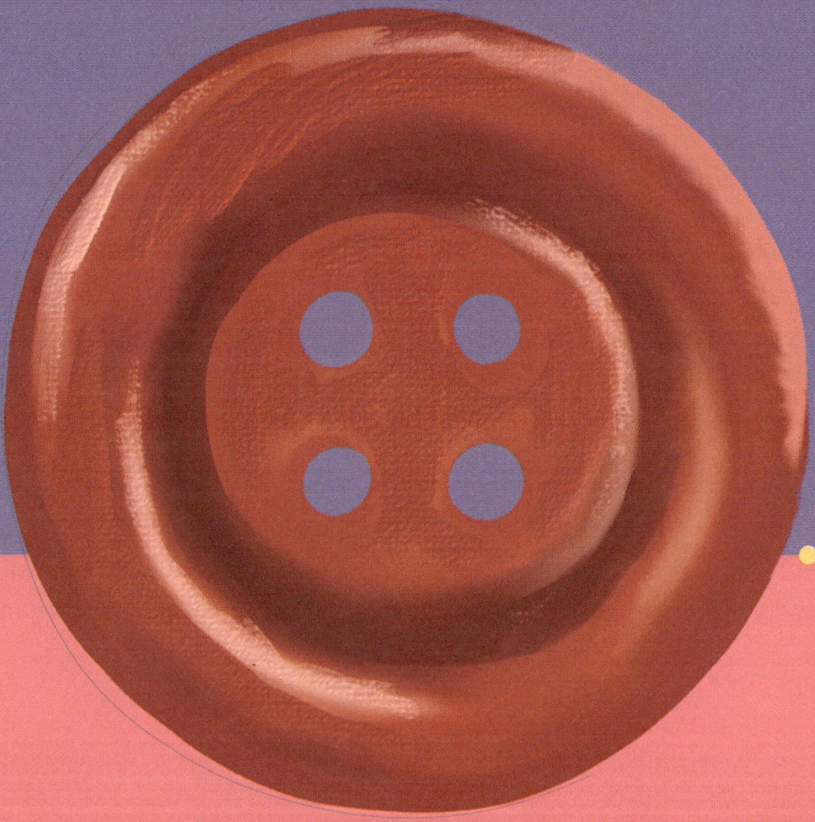

Now let's make some dots!

It could not be easier.
Just dip the tip of your
finger in paint and
touch this paper.

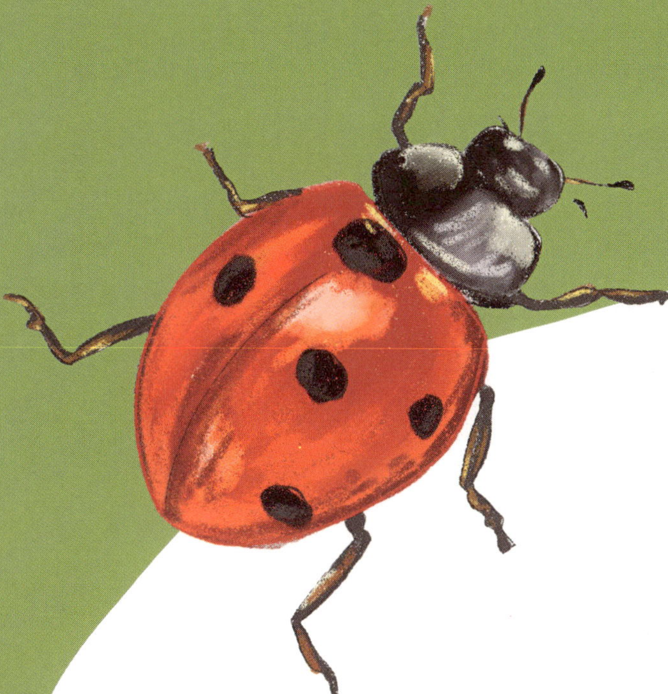

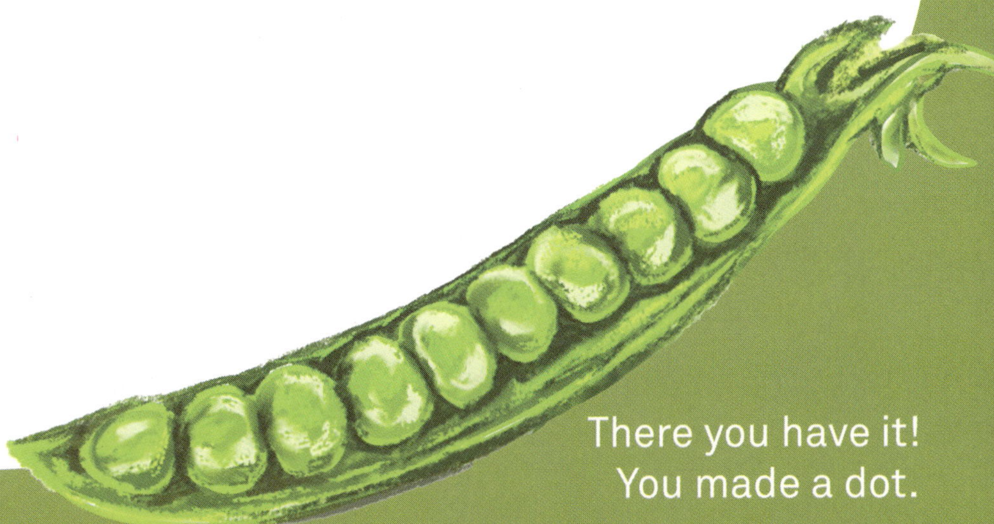

There you have it!
You made a dot.

Yayoi Kusama is a Japanese artist who grew up on a pumpkin farm. Ever since she was a little girl, she loved painting. She imagined her world as a canvas of tiny, colourful dots.

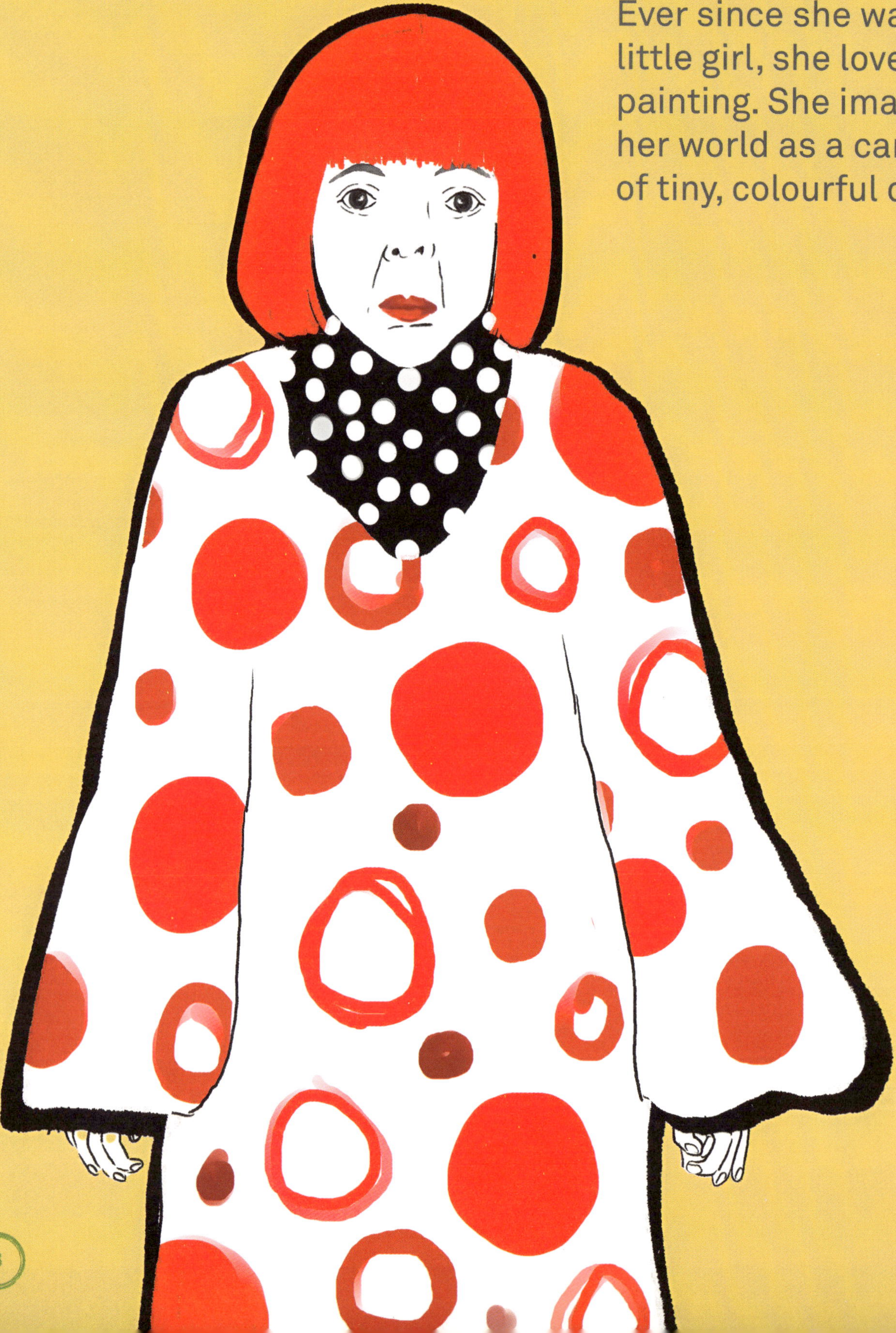

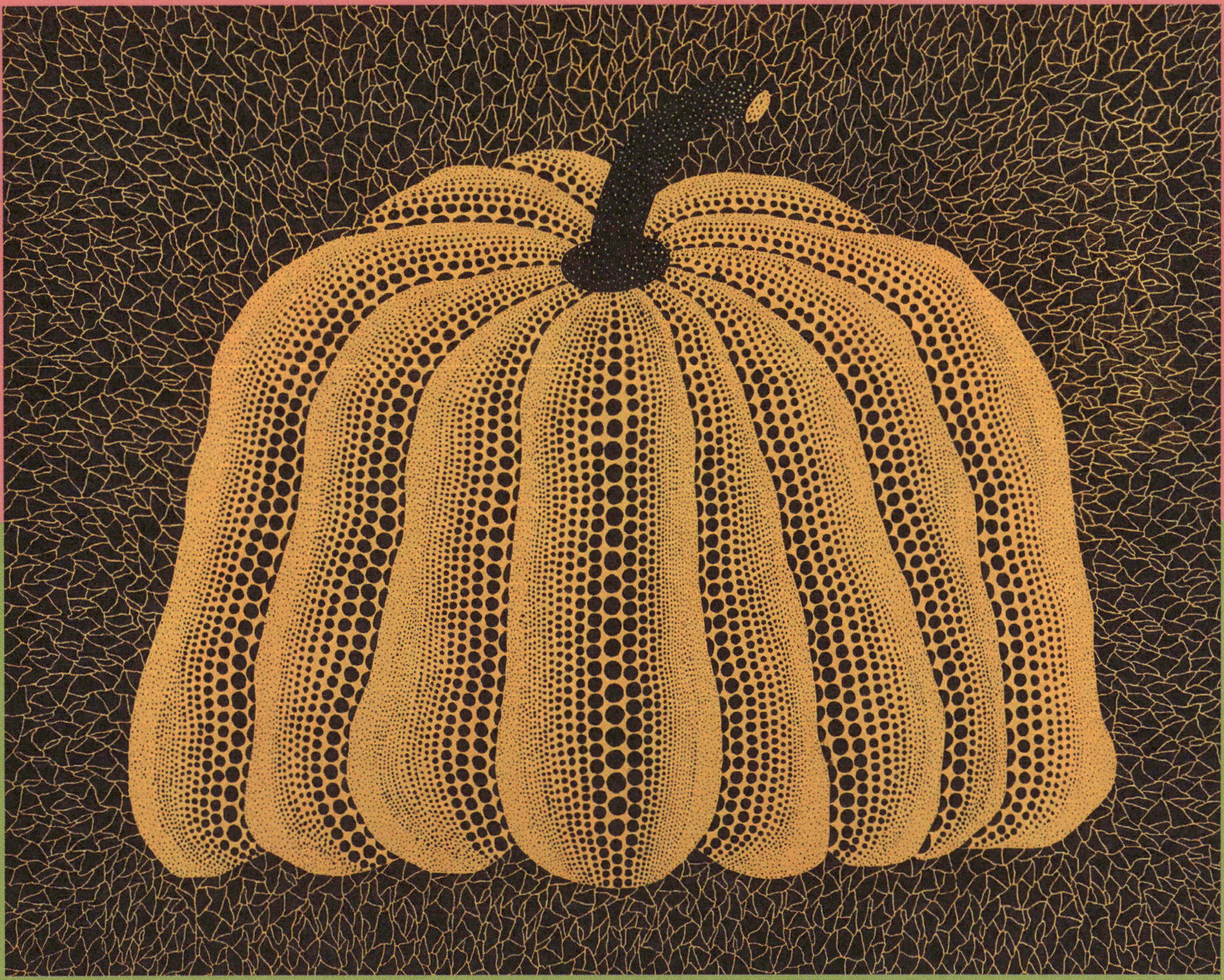

Artist: Yayoi Kusama

She covers everything with dots—sculptures, paintings, even entire rooms, from floor to ceiling!

What do you think when you see this yellow pumpkin with its many rows of polka dots? Did you notice the pattern in the background?

Yayoi painted flowers, butterflies and mushrooms too, but pumpkins were her favourite.

This is Sonali. She visited the Yayoi Kusama Museum in Tokyo.

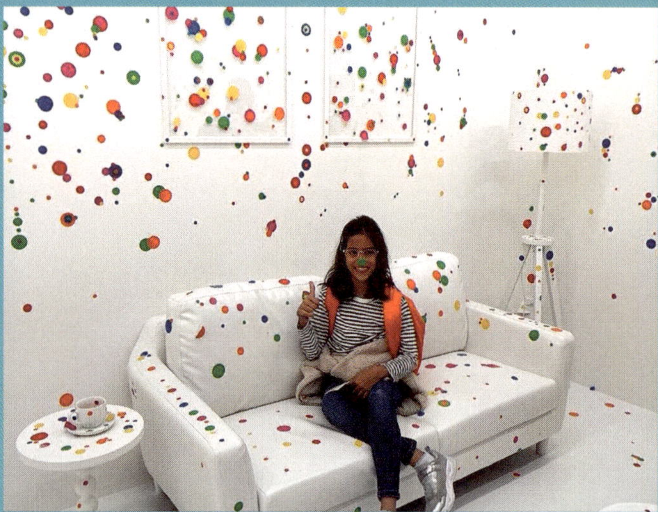

They had a white room filled with white furniture and invited visitors to stick polka dots all over it.

Like Sonali, you can fill this room with dots too—it's fun!

You can use the back of a pen or a pencil, a twig, or even a Q-tip to make dots. Dip it in any thick paint like acrylic, poster or tempera and then quickly press it on the picture.

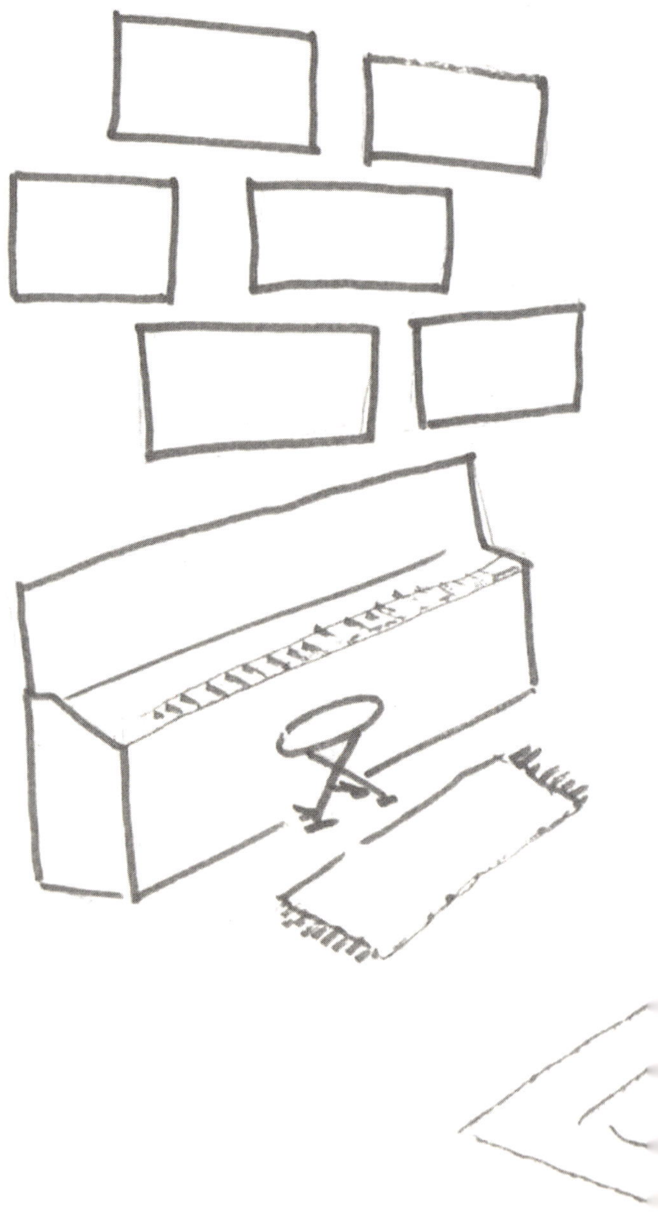

Let's fill the room with dots.
It's a dot explosion!

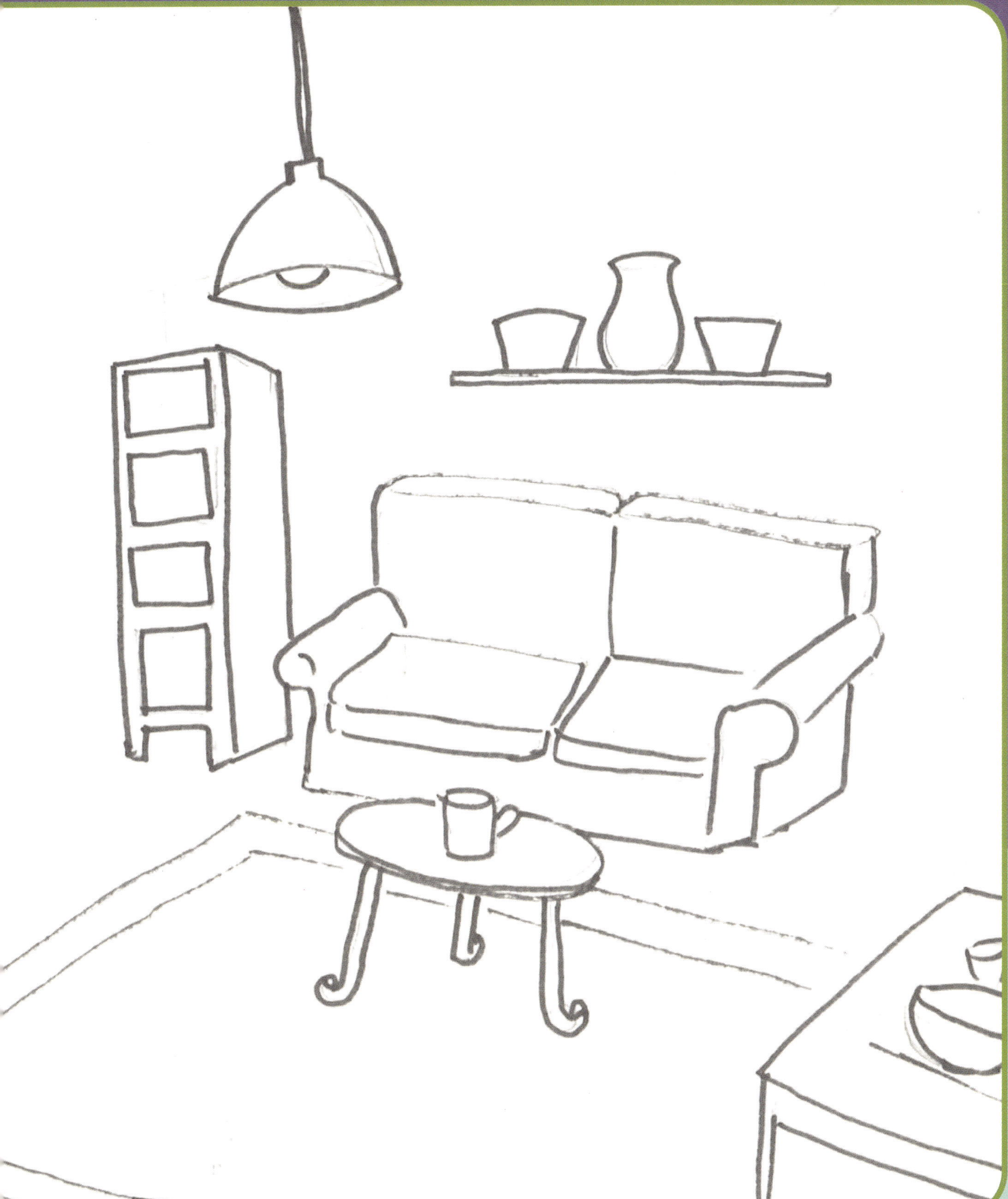

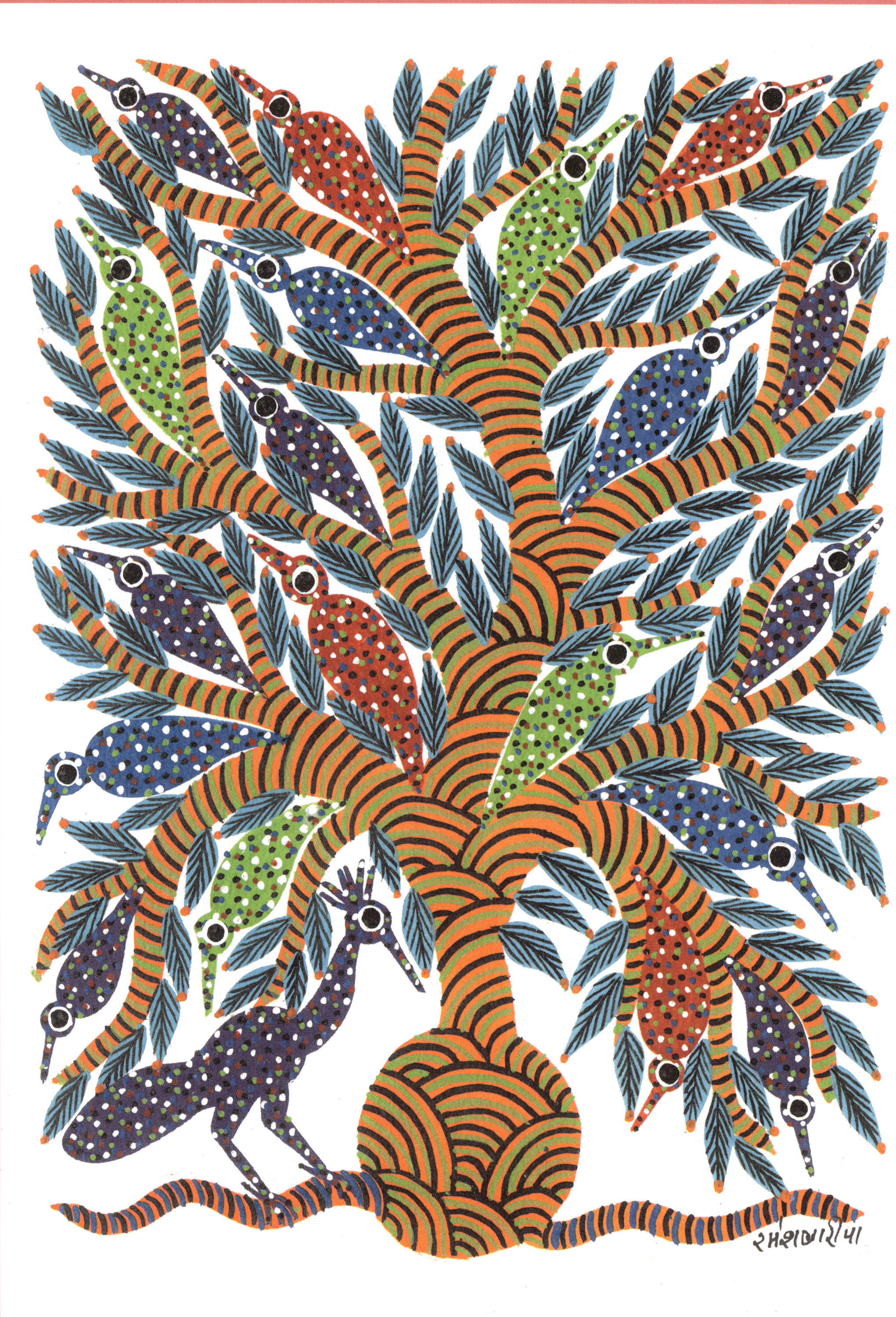
રમેશબારીયા

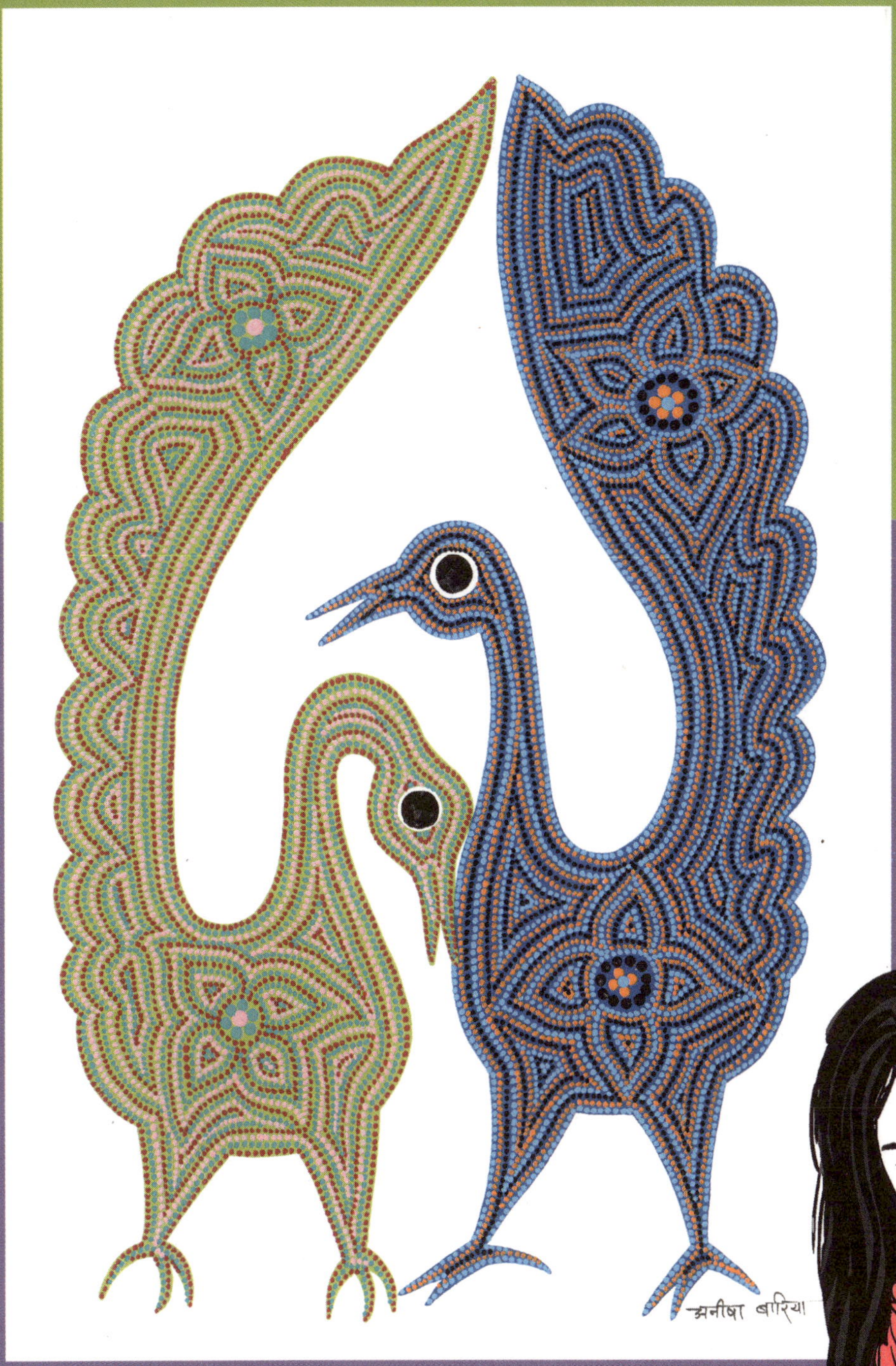

Anisha Bareeya is an artist from the Bhil tribe in India. She has been painting since she was eleven years old.

Bhil artists paint trees, animals and birds that they see around them.

Do you see how she uses many small dots in neat rows to fill these birds?

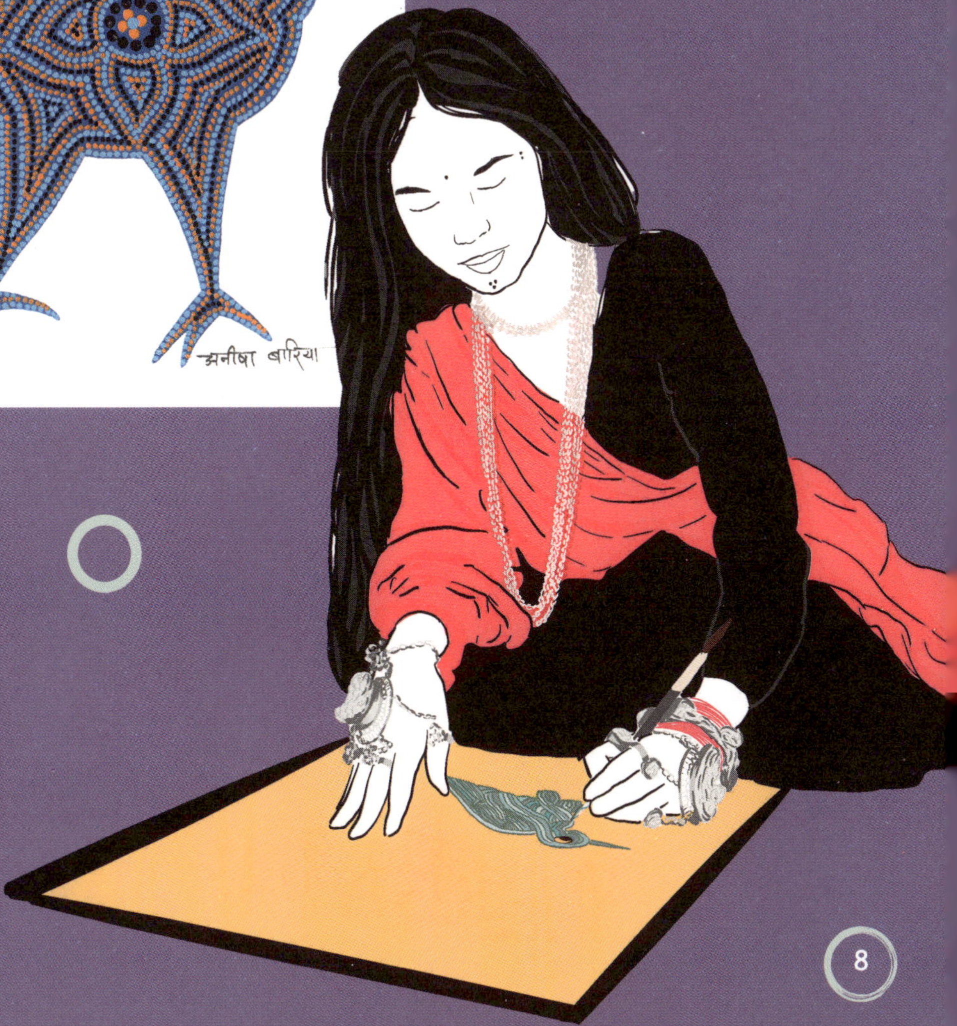

Anisha drew two more birds for you to fill with dots.

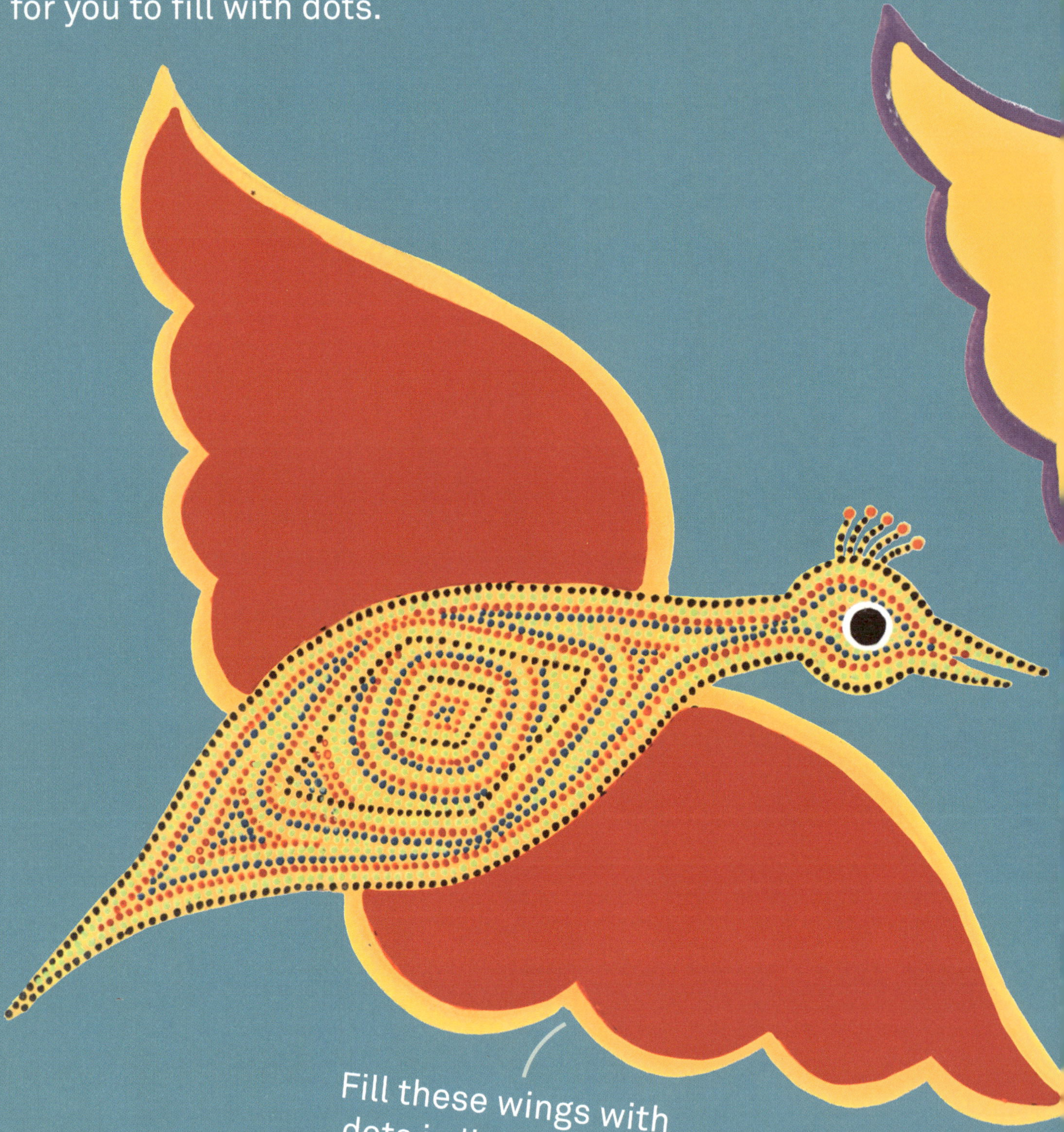

Fill these wings with dots in bright colours like green, blue or red.

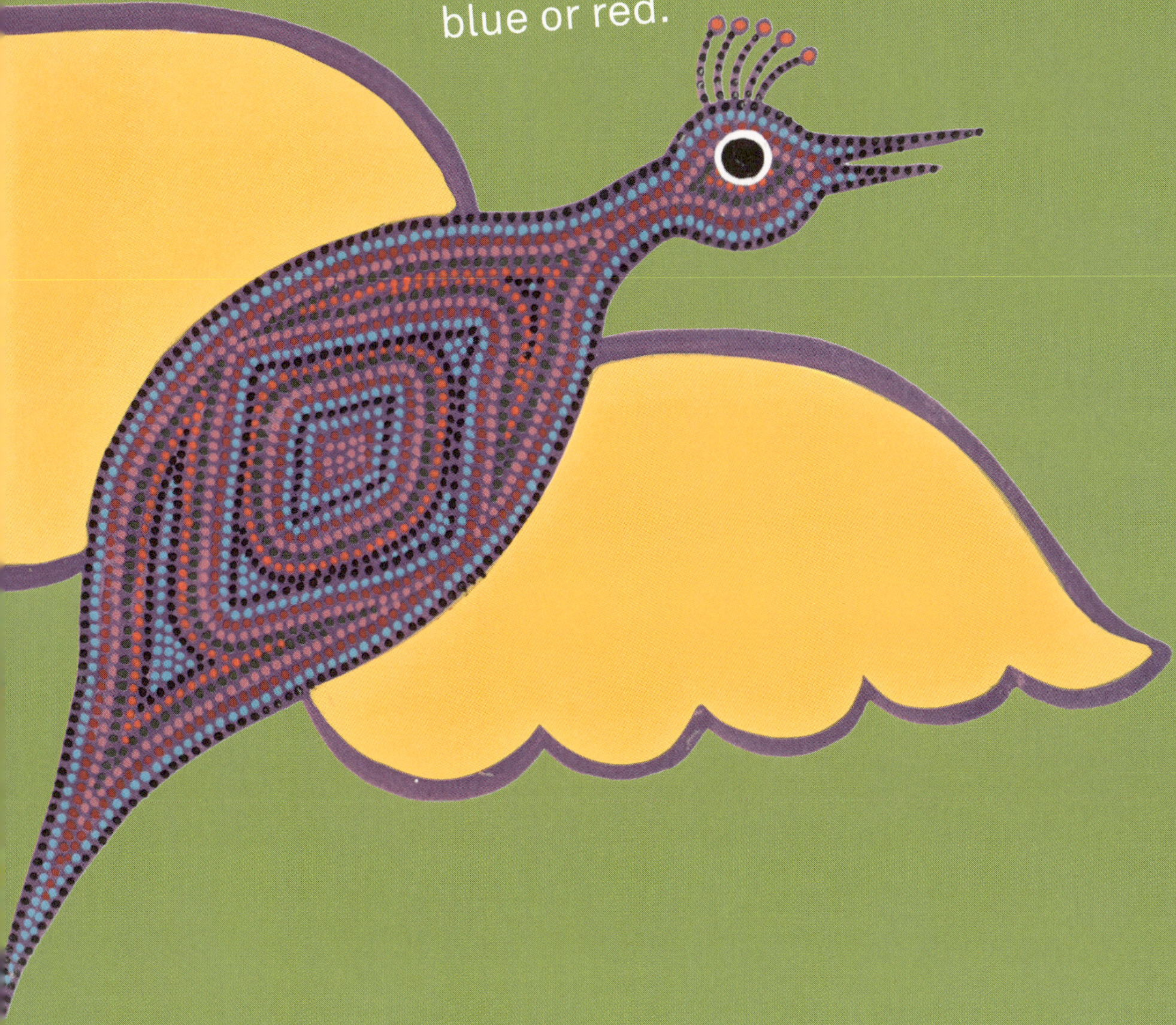

ART SUPPLIES: Acrylic, poster or tempera paint, a bowl of water (and your finger)

Lines of All Kinds

We learnt that when we make a tiny
mark with our pencil, it's called a dot.
If we continue moving our pencil, we make a LINE!

Here are some trees painted by the Indian artist **Chameli Ramachandran** using just lines.

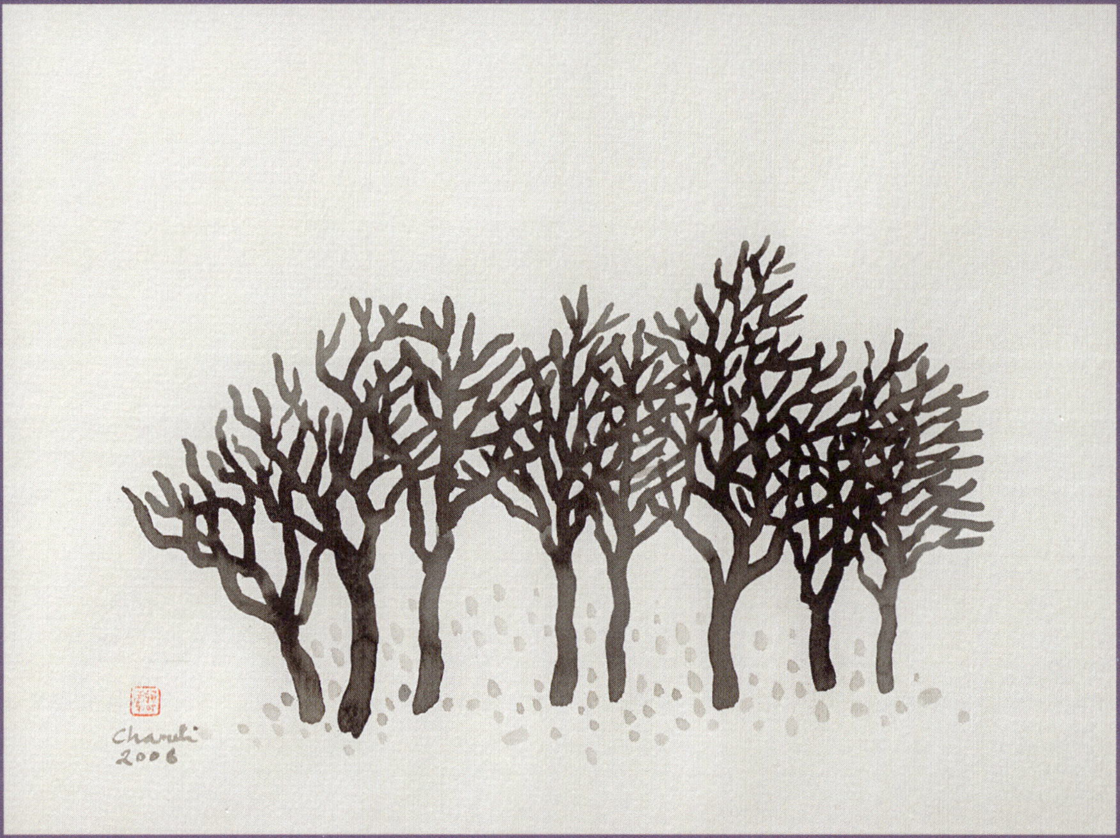

We can use lines to draw anything.
Lines can be curvy or wavy, long or short, thick or thin.

Chameli loves to paint with a Chinese brush and ink.

Chameli's father was a teacher, so she grew up in a beautiful college campus in Bengal called Shantiniketan. The campus was surrounded by trees.

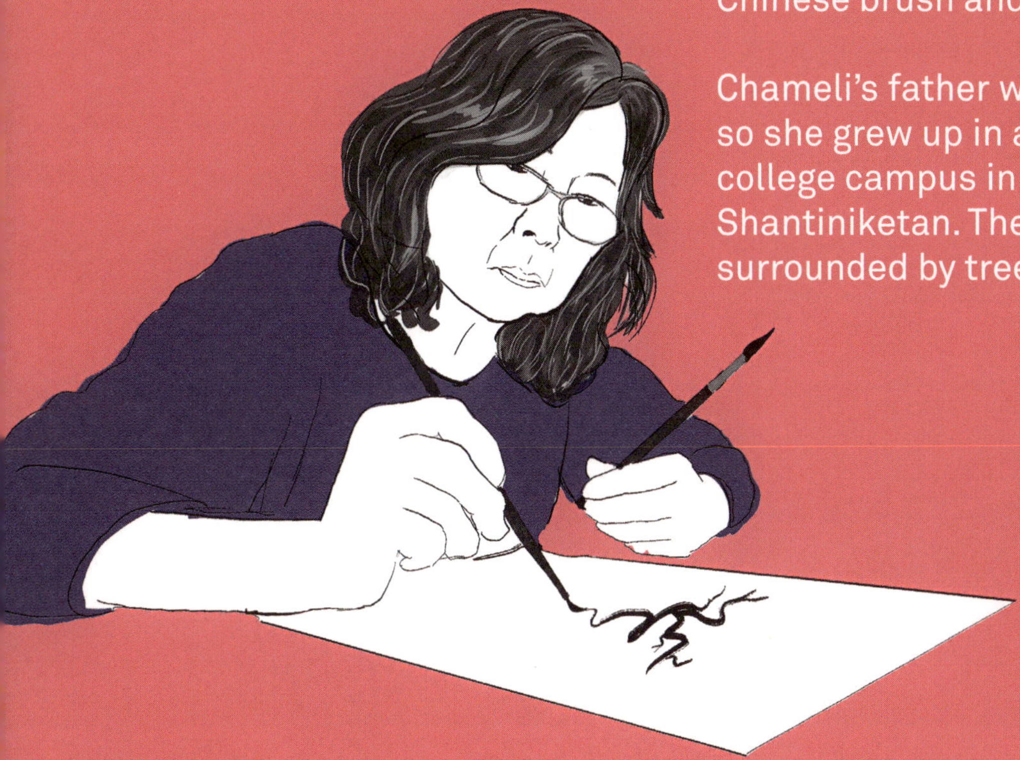

Do you like trees? What kind of trees do you see around you?

As trees grow older, their trunks grow thicker and they have more branches that spread out in all directions.

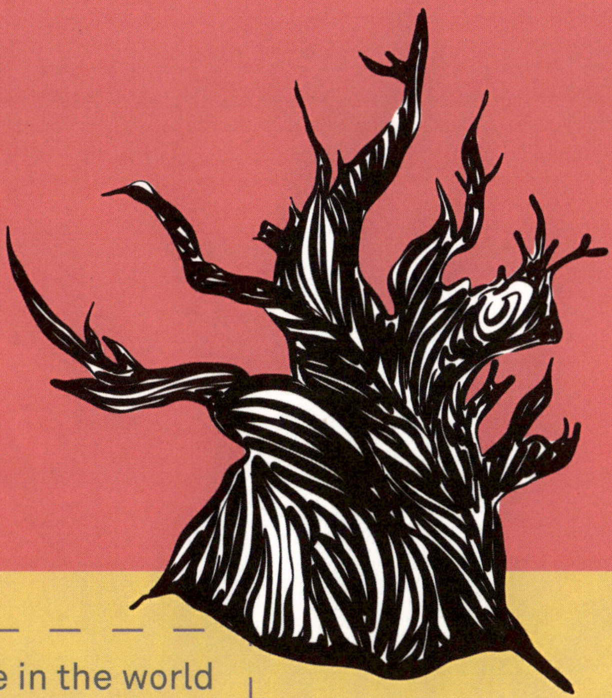

Did you know the oldest tree in the world is a special kind of Pine in California. It is almost 5000 years old!

See how Chameli uses many lines to
make this big beautiful tree.
Would you like to make one too?

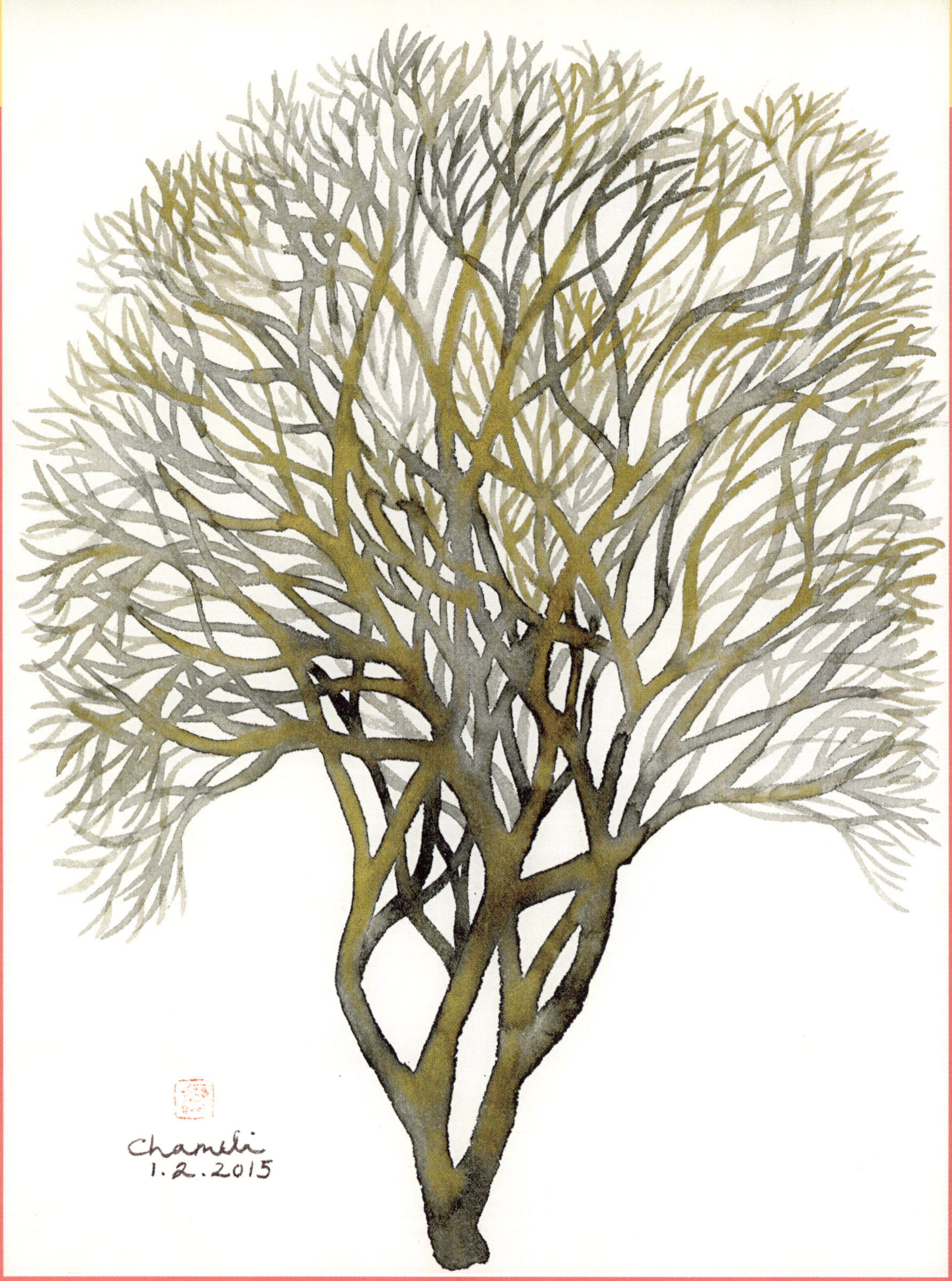

Take an oil pastel and let's start practising lines here. You could add branches to this tree.

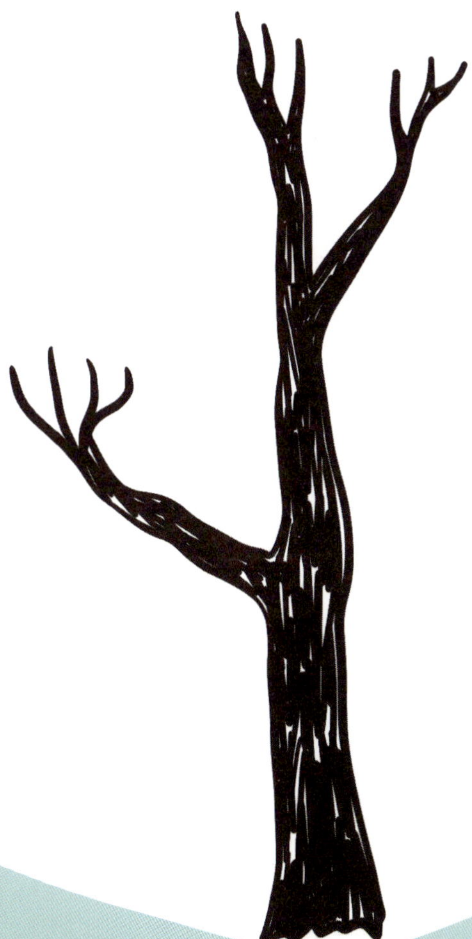

Finger Painted Flowers

We see flowers every day.
On trees, in gardens and in parks.

Red, orange, yellow and purple are bright colours that we often see in flowers.

Today, we will paint a garden full of flowers using our fingers instead of a brush!

Are you ready to get started?

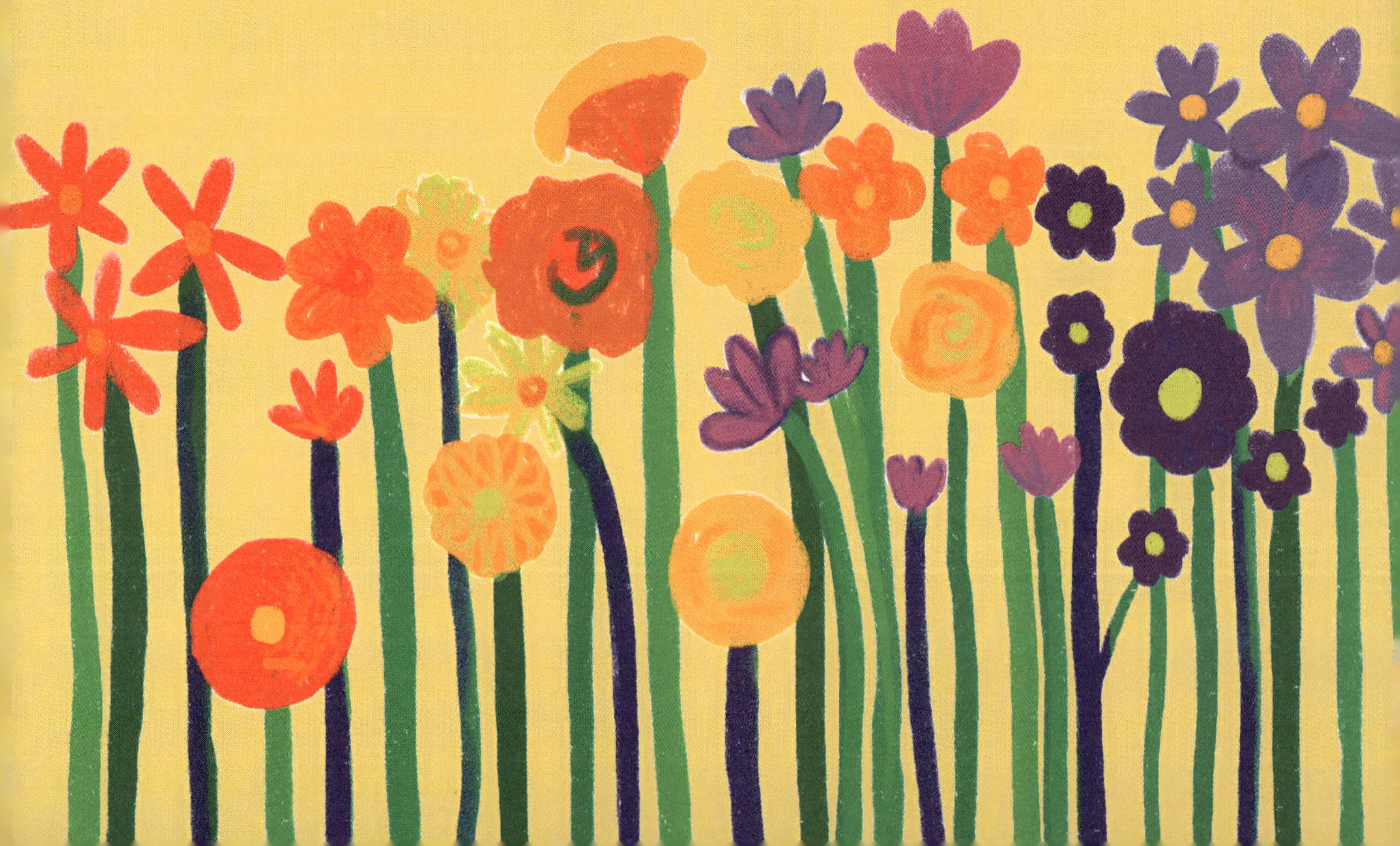

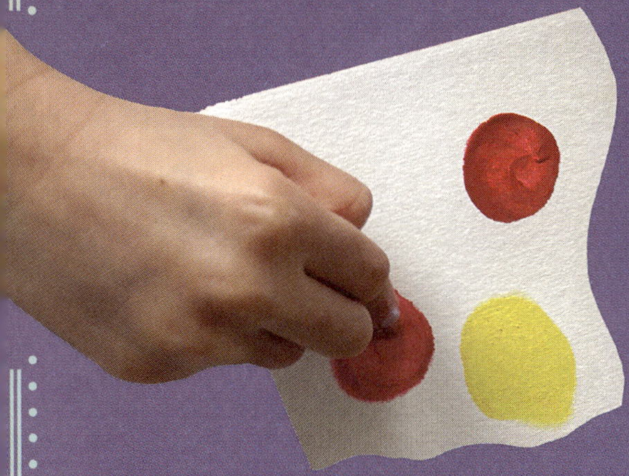

Dip the tip of your finger in water and then in any bright colour paint. Move it in a small circle to make a round shape. This will become your flower.

Let's fill the top of the paper with flowers.

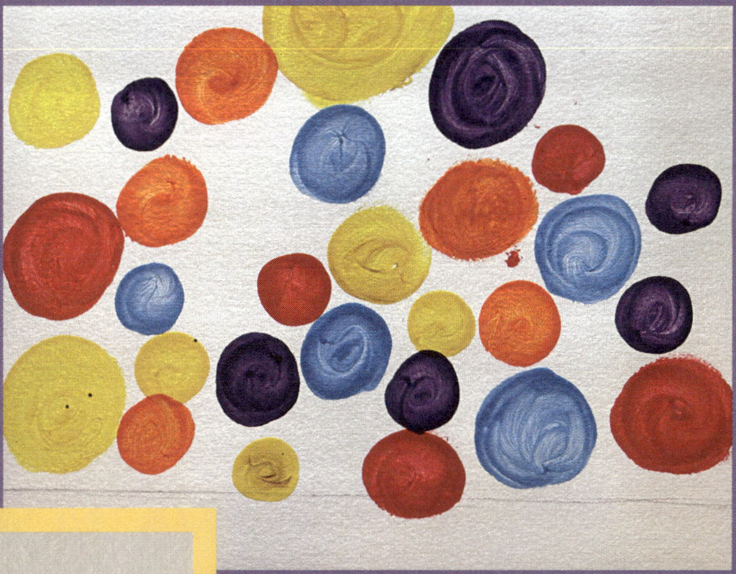

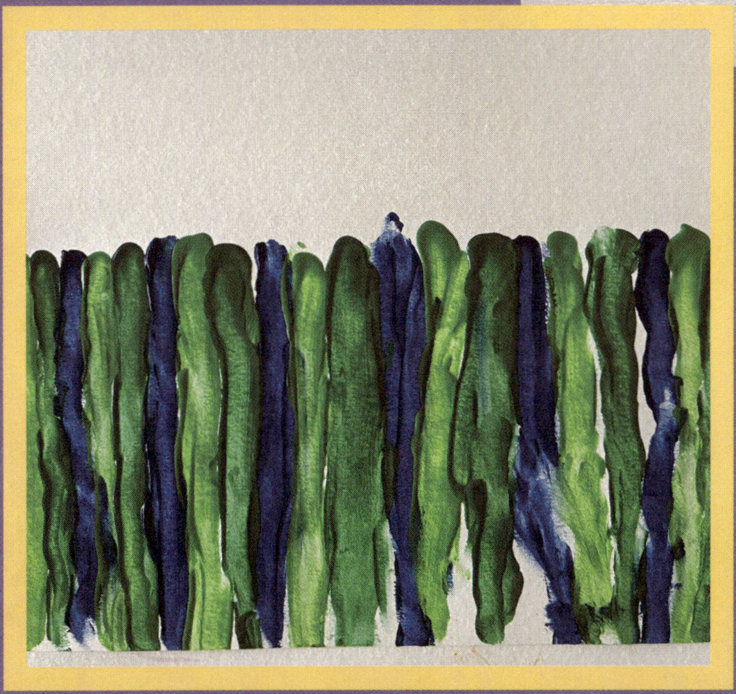

To make your stems, dip the tip of your finger in light green, dark green or even blue paint and make a long line on the paper.

After the flowers are dry, you can add a dot of a different colour in the middle of each flower.

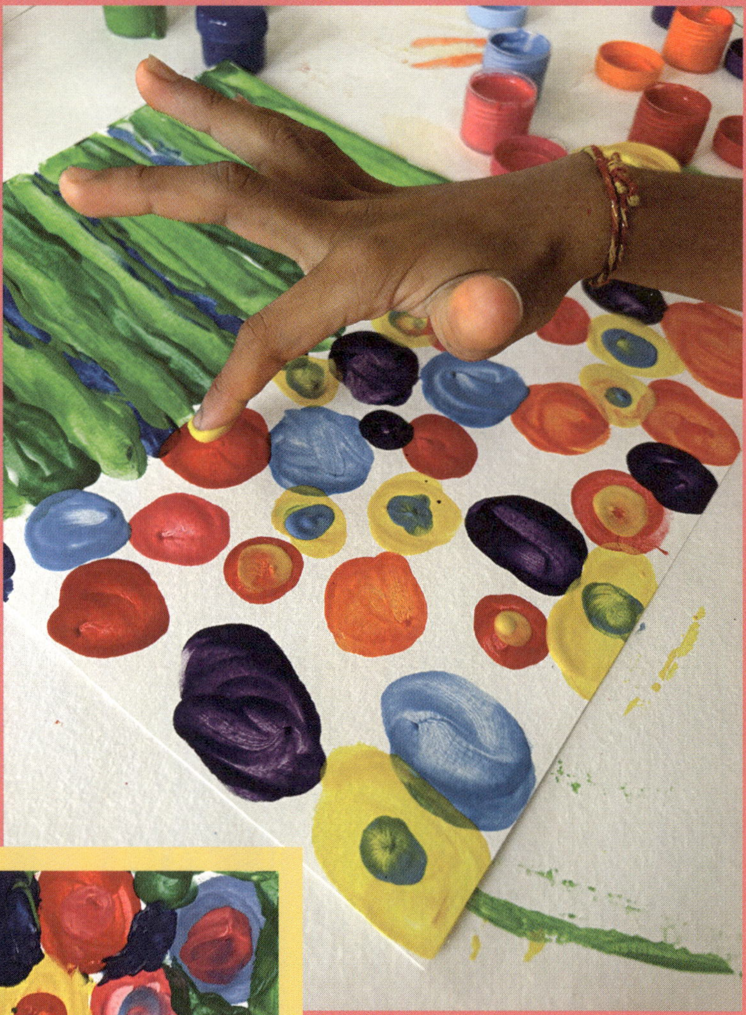

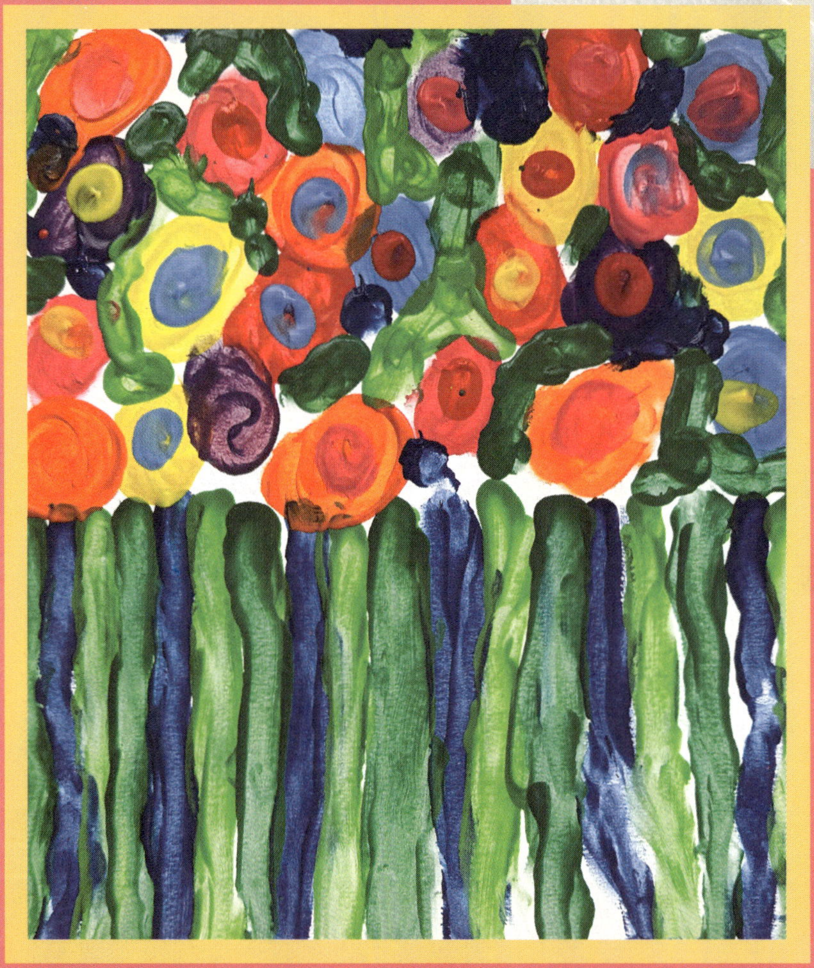

Finally, take a look at your work and fill in any white spaces around the flowers with green paint.

Would you like to make your own garden filled with bright flowers here?

ART SUPPLIES: Acrylic, poster or tempera paint, bowl of water (and your finger)

Pattern Power

When you draw the same kind of line many times, you create a PATTERN.

We see patterns all around us—on a shell at the beach, on the clothes we wear or on the wings of a butterfly.

Can you complete the patterns in these boxes?

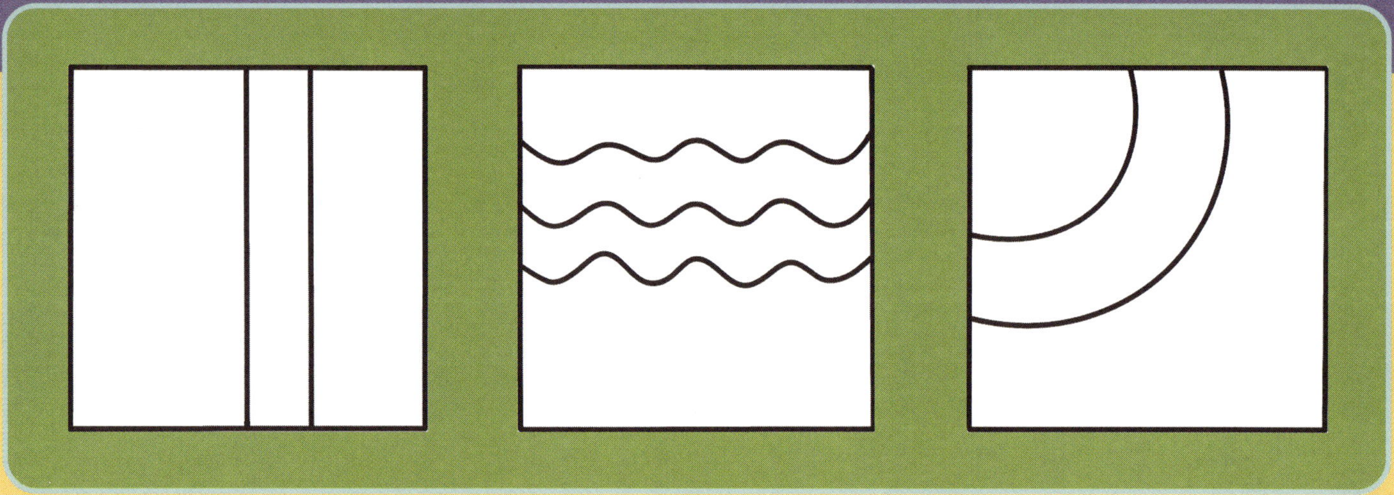

Meet **Kailash Kumar Pradhan**, an artist from the Gond tribe. He lives in a village called Patangarh. His parents are farmers. Kailash grew up surrounded by art in his village.

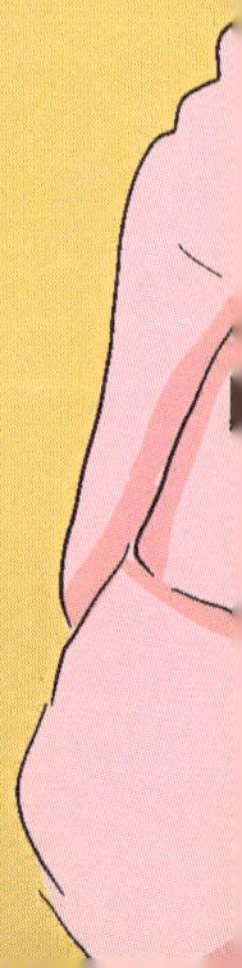

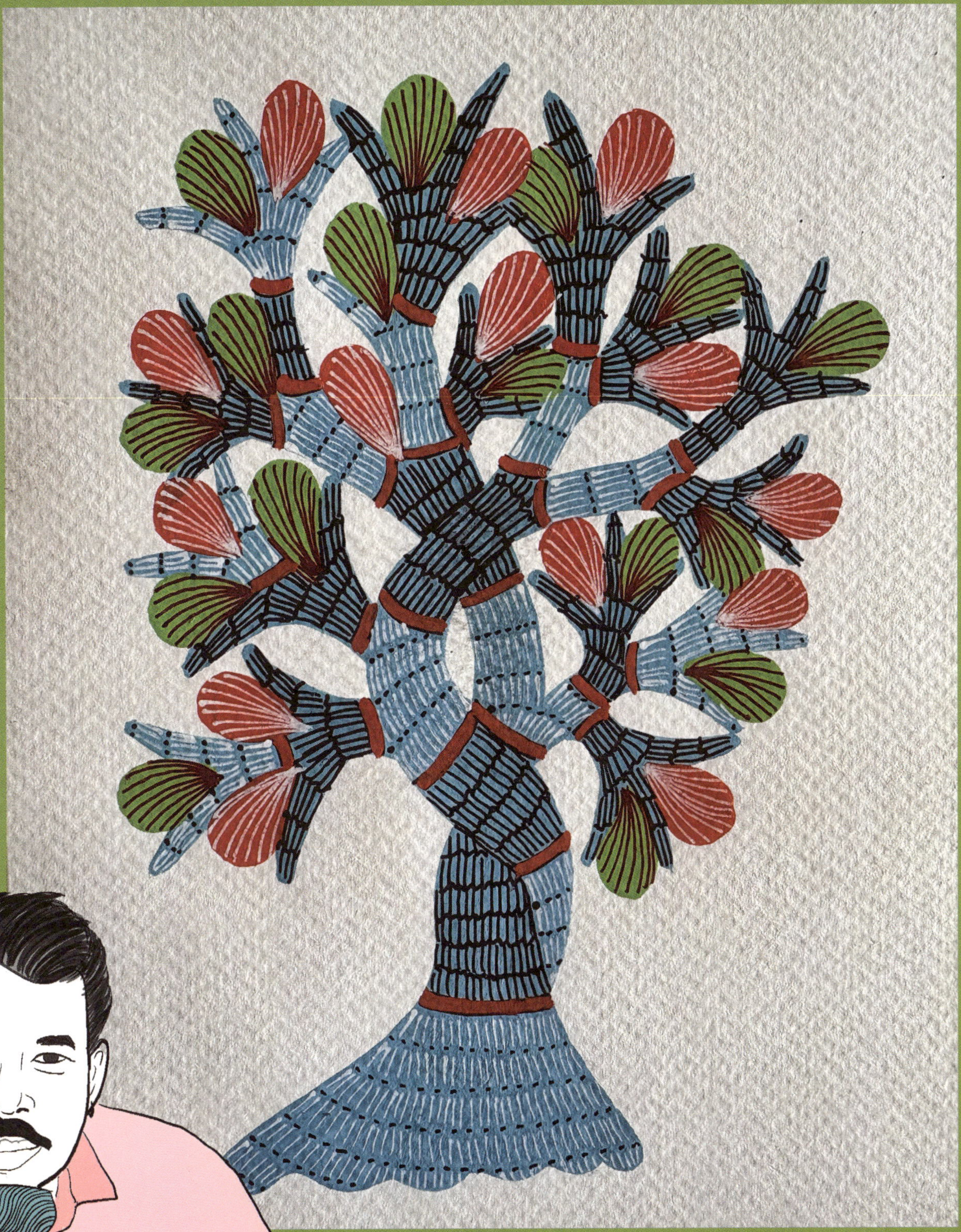

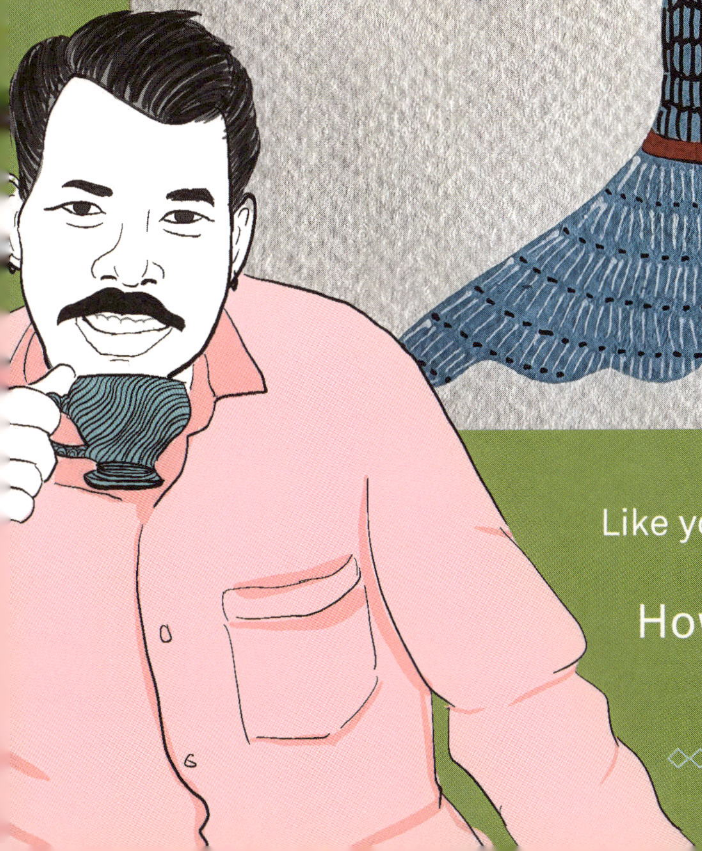

Here's a beautiful tree Kailash made.
Like you, he made patterns using just lines.

How many different patterns do you see in the tree?

Do you see how Kailash invents patterns using just simple lines?

Kailash calls this pattern Chher-Chhera. He makes it by just drawing four lines. Doesn't it look like a star?

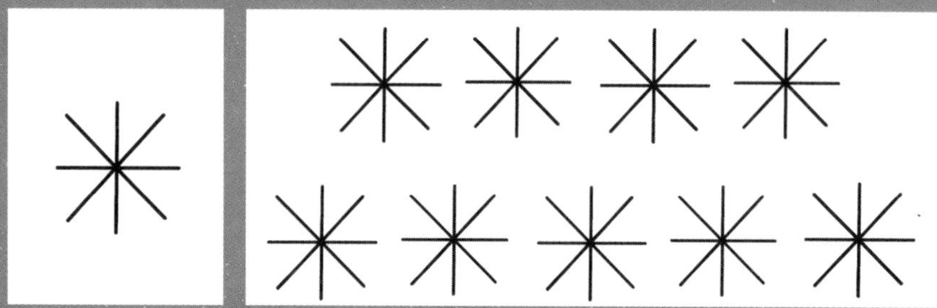

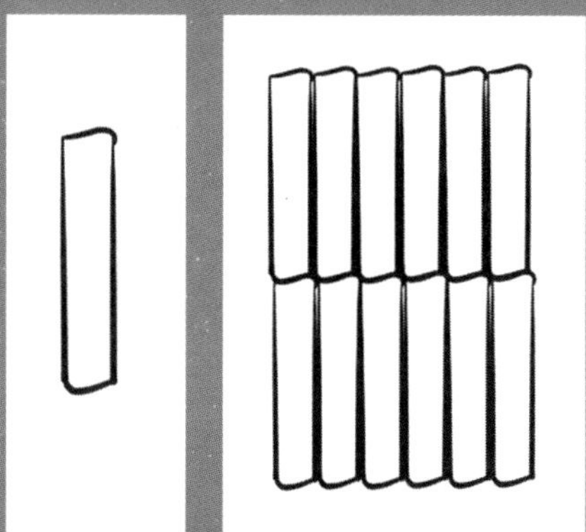

He named this pattern Khaddar because it reminds him of the dried grass used to make the roofs of houses in his village.

The Parsa Paan pattern looks like a leaf he sees every day.

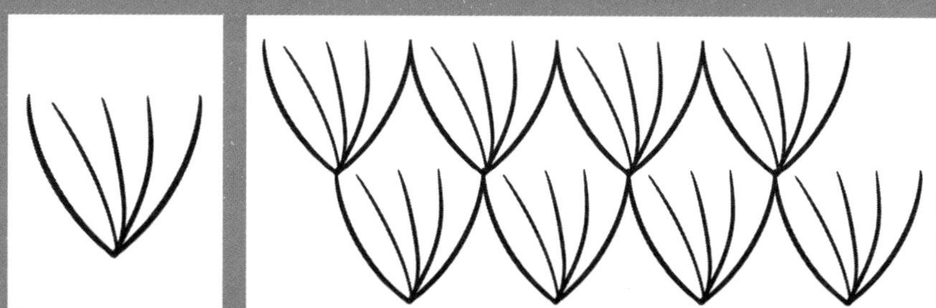

Now it's time for you to make your own patterns. Kailash needs your help to complete his elephant. Fill in the blank orange and yellow parts using your own patterns.

ART SUPPLIES: Pencil or black pen

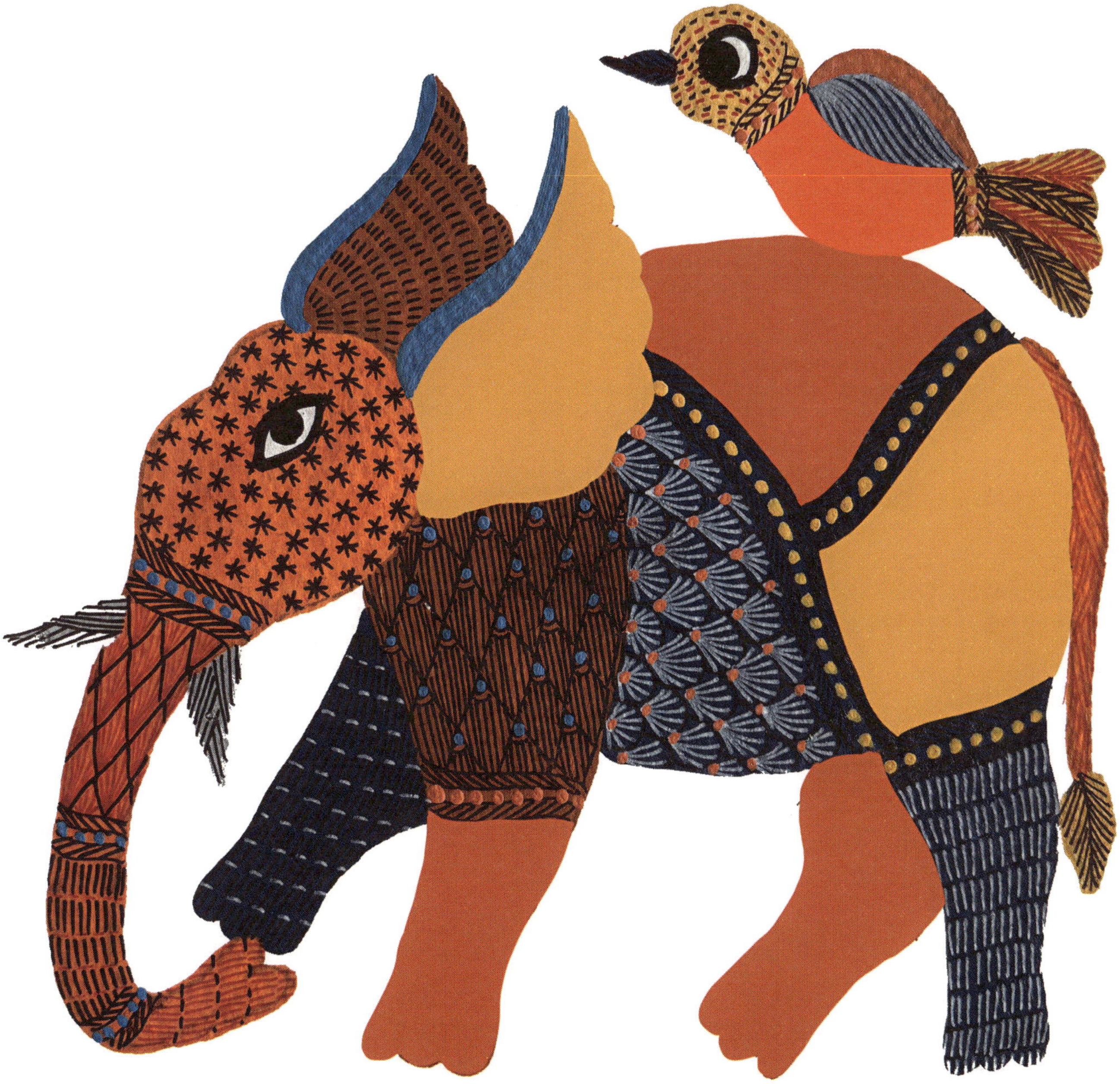

Texture Explorers

TEXTURE is how something feels when you touch it. Fur is soft, rocks are rough, tree trunks are bumpy.

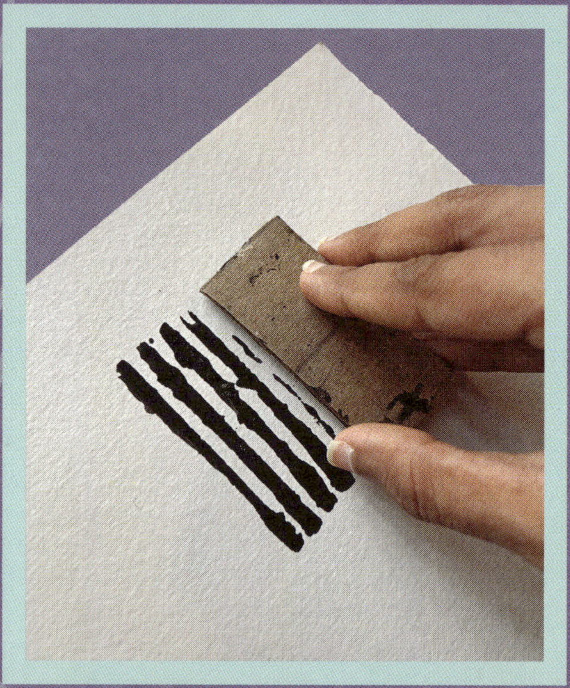

Let's try something new. Paint a piece of bumpy cardboard using thick paint.

Before the paint dries, quickly press it hard onto blank paper. What do you see?

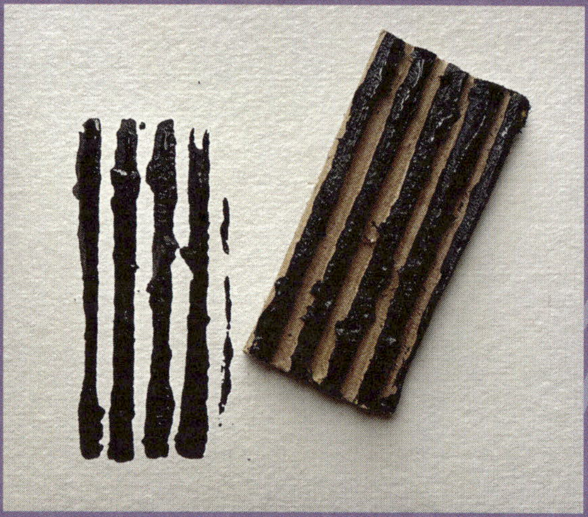

Some of the paint stays stuck to the cardboard but the part that appears on the paper is called a PRINT.

What else can we use to create prints? How about an orange peel? A pot scrubber?

Now you are a texture explorer! Pick an object with an interesting texture and paint it with a dark colour. Quickly press your object in the white boxes before the paint dries.

You can fill each box with a different kind of print. See how we can make an interesting artwork with just textures!

ART SUPPLIES: Acrylic, poster or tempera paint, bowl of water, thick brush and many objects with bumpy textures

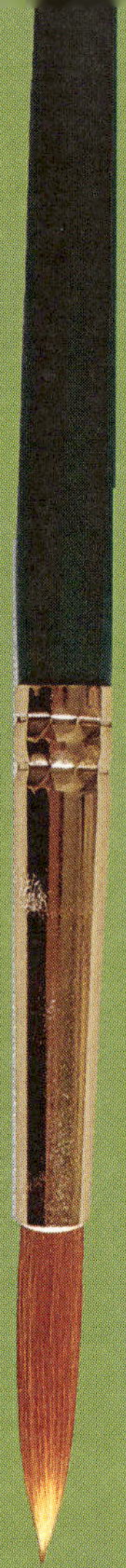

How to Paint

1 Fill a cup with clean water and keep it near your paints. Choose a thick brush and hold the lower shiny metal part of it, like you would hold a pencil.

2 Dip the soft part of the paintbrush in water, and gently press it on the side of the cup to squeeze out any extra water. We do this to make sure that the paper doesn't become soggy.

3 Next, load up the brush with paint by putting its soft end on the watercolour cake and swirling it about. Now you touch the paint on your paper and that's it ...

You are painting!

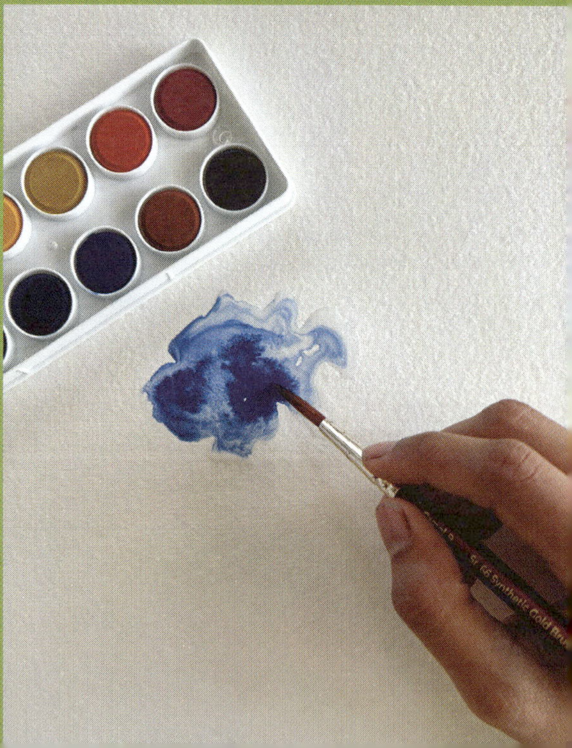

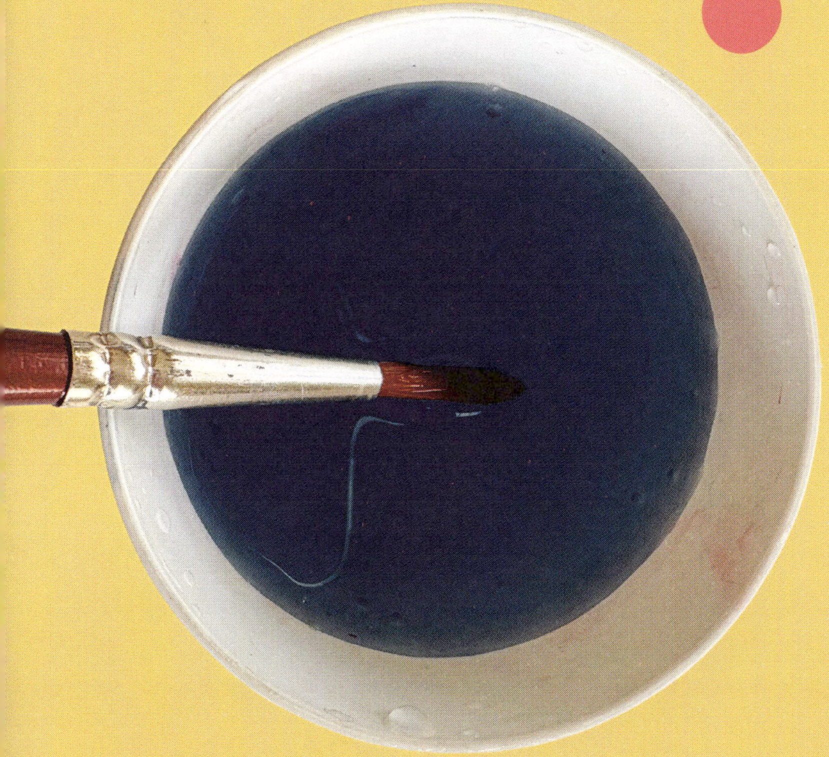

PRO TIP

When you want to use a new colour, remember to dip your brush in the water cup and give it a quick wash till it is clean.

If you skip this step, your colours will get mixed up.

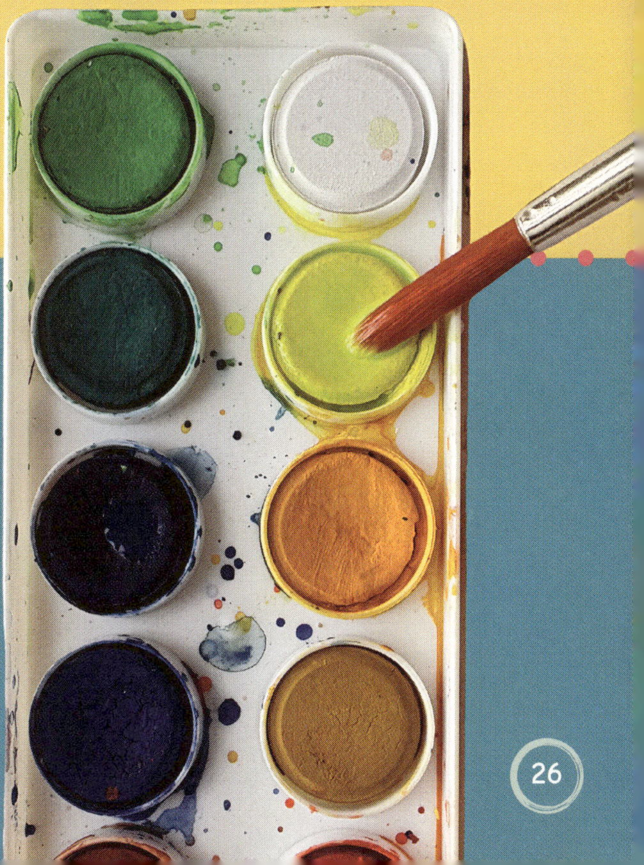

When your paint cake becomes messy, you can use your paintbrush and water to clean it.

Oil Pastel Resist

Have you ever tried painting outlines or tiny patterns using a paintbrush? It can be quite tricky! Here is a fun and easy way to do it.

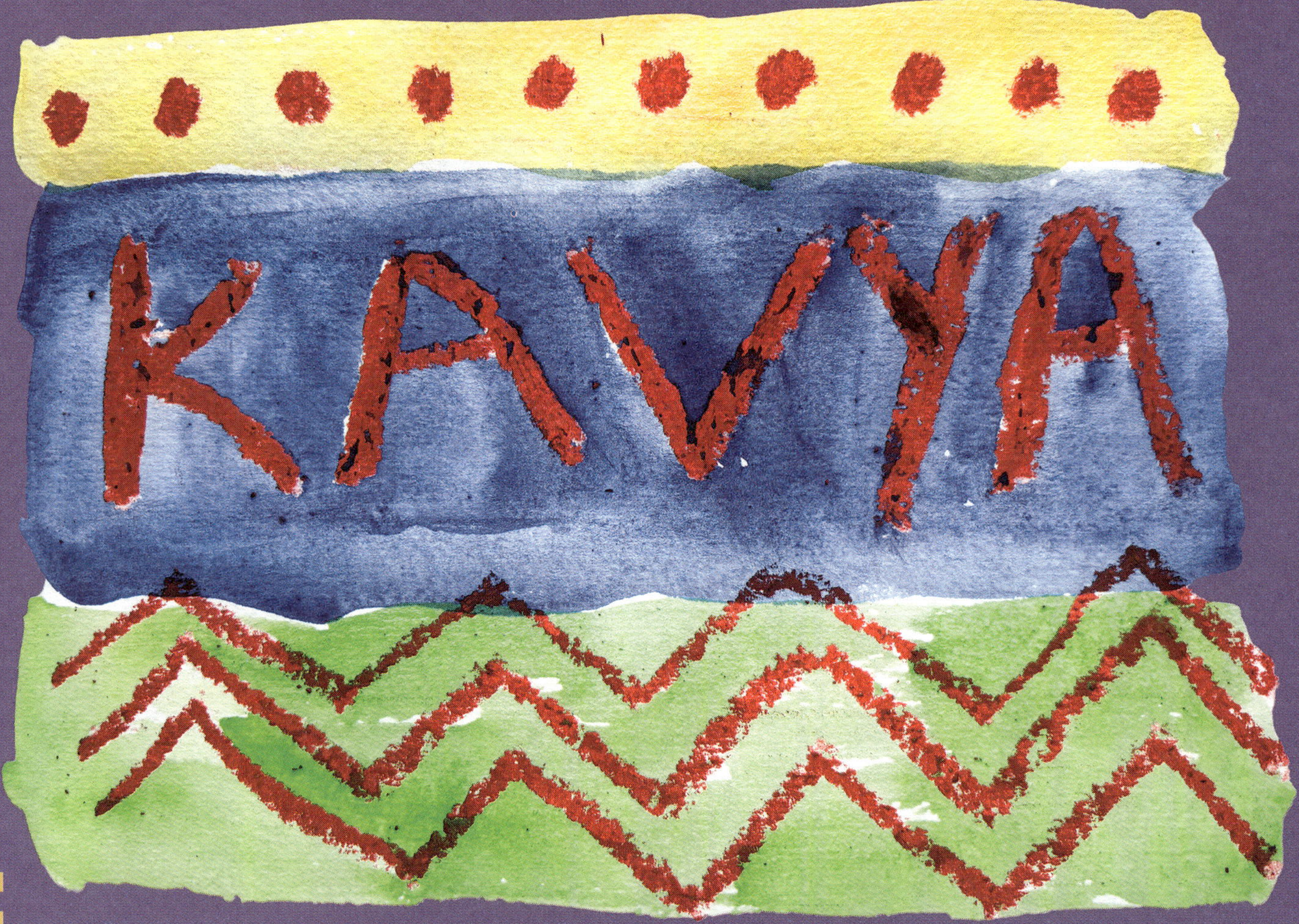

First, use an oil pastel in any dark colour like red, blue, purple, green to write your name. You can make dots, lines or patterns above or below it. Paint over the oil pastel drawings using watercolours. You'll see the patterns and outlines remain uncovered by the paint. The oil in the pastel pushes away water. That's called OIL PASTEL RESIST.

Isn't that a surprise?

It's your turn to practise the oil pastel magic trick. Write your name really big using a dark coloured oil pastel. You can make patterns around it. Remember to press the oil pastel down firmly. Now paint over it using watercolour paints.

ART SUPPLIES: Oil pastels, watercolours, thick brush, bowl of water

Colours of the Sun

Two artists, **Doyel Joshi and Neil Ghose Balser** came up with a beautiful art installation for the Brighton Arts Festival. The theme of the festival was 'A New Dawn.'

They collected 6000 paintings of the sun made by young artists like you, and displayed them all together on the walls inside an old building. Doesn't that look like one huge wonderful artwork?

Most of the paintings used red, pink, orange and yellow. These are the colours of fire or the sun, and are called WARM COLOURS.

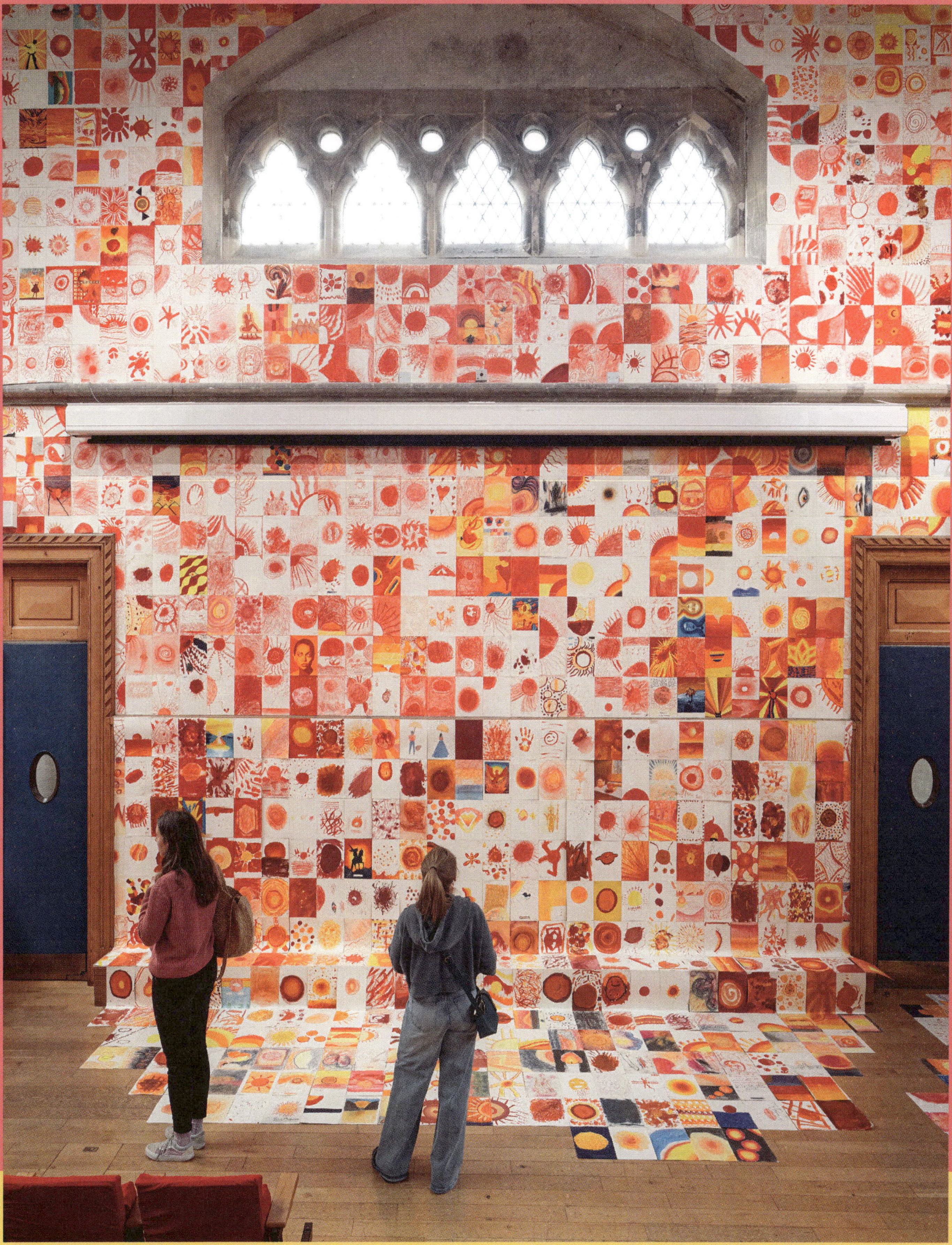

Artists: Doyel Joshi and Neil Ghose Balser

Shall we draw our own sun?

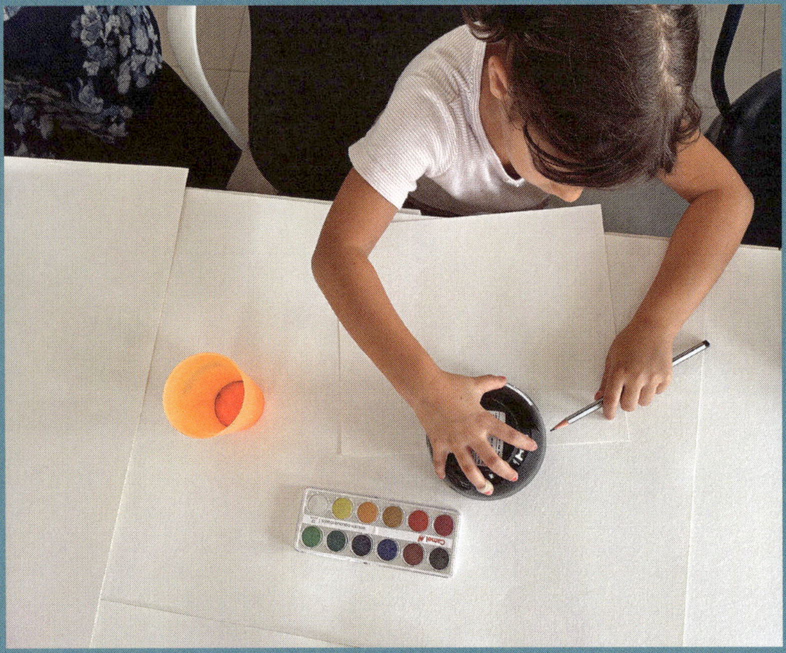

Turn over a bowl and trace around it to get a circle or semi-circle anywhere on the page.

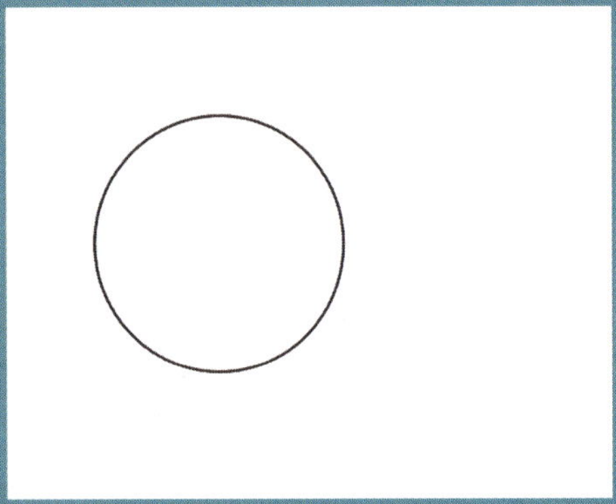

Where will you choose to position the centre of your sun?

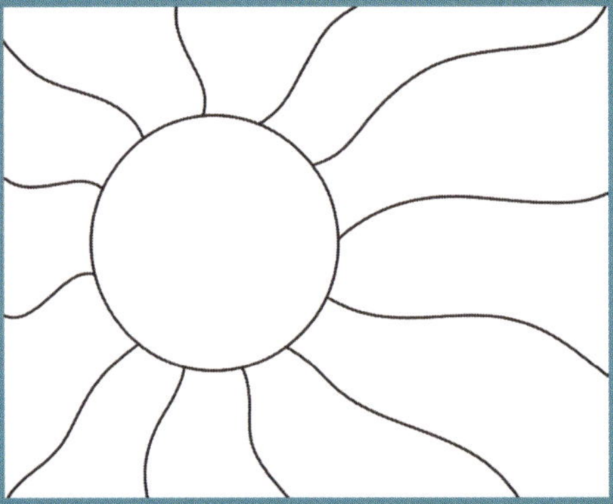

You could use straight lines, zig-zag lines or different shapes for the rays.

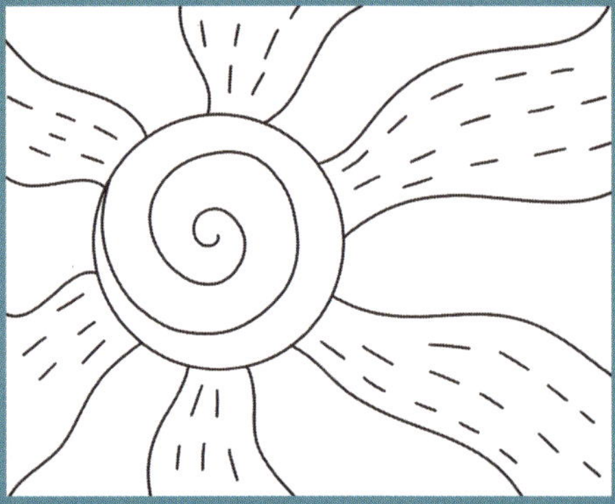

Next add short broken lines, dots, swirls or other simple patterns.

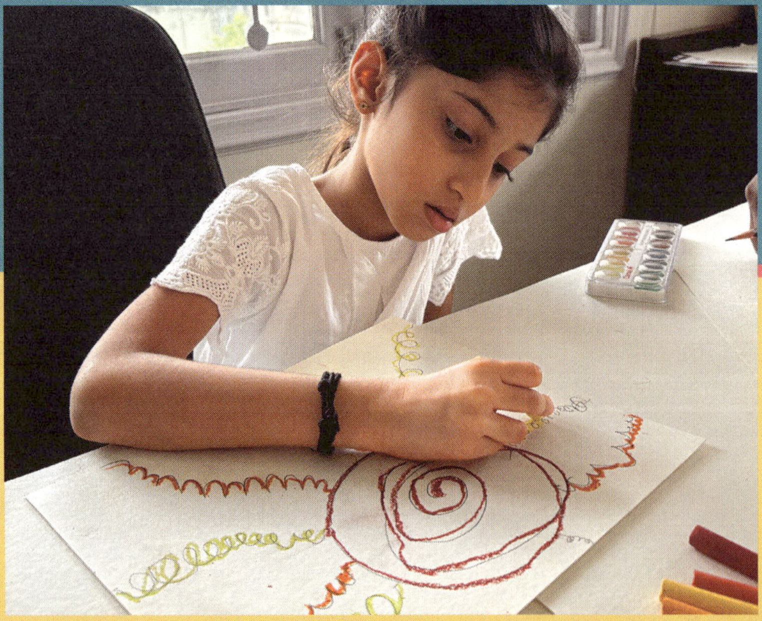

Are you ready to colour?

Outline all your pencil lines and patterns using oil pastels and then use paint to fill the empty spaces.

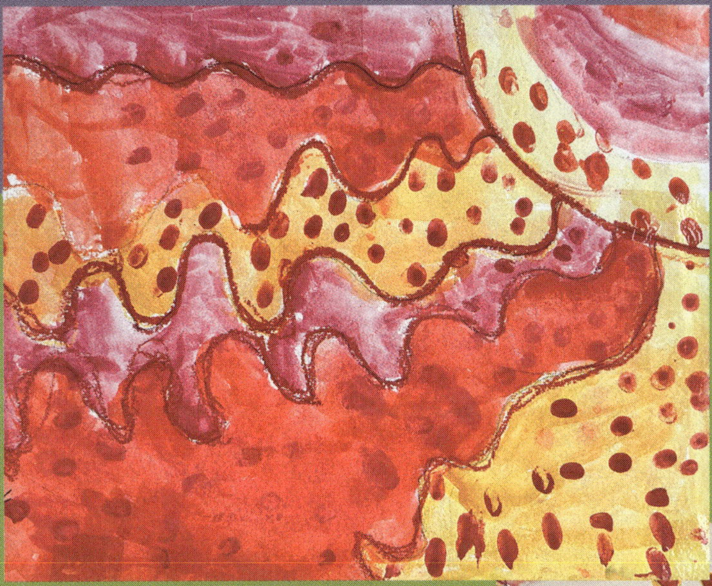

Don't forget that warm colours like red, pink, orange and yellow are the colours of the sun.

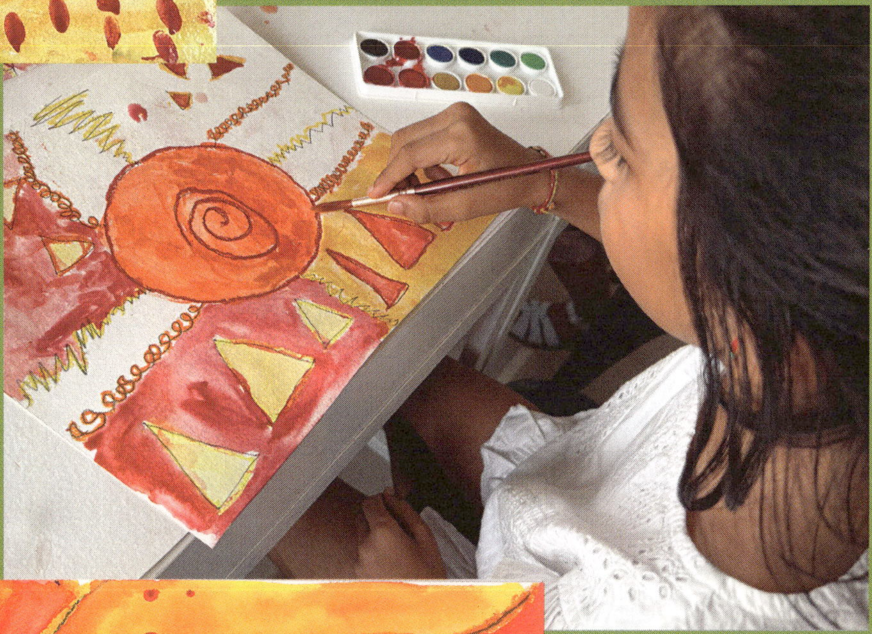

Take a moment to plan your colours!

Maybe all the yellows first, then wash your brush and move on to the reds?

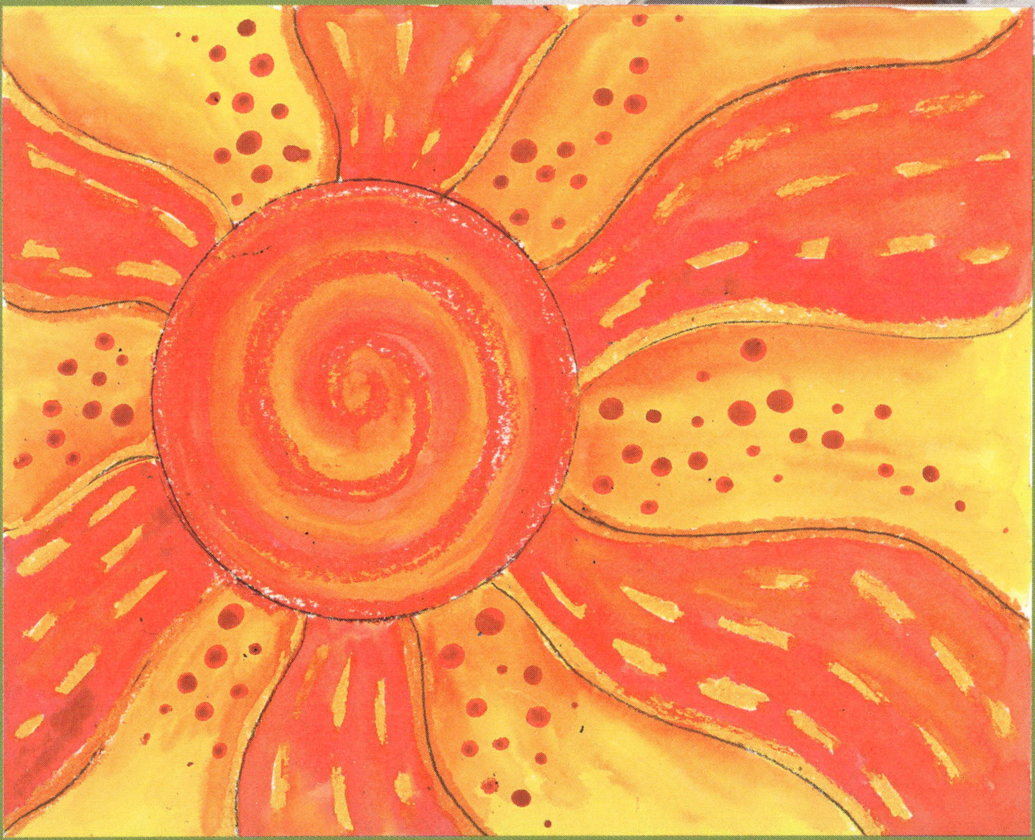

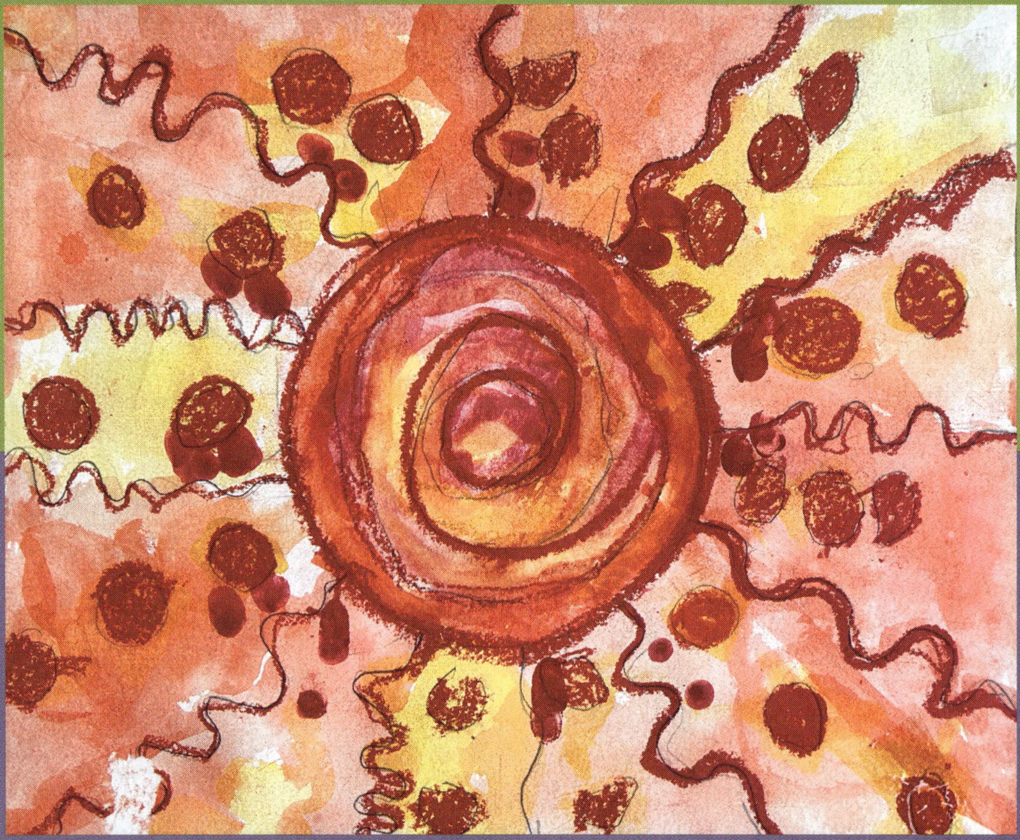

Do you see that even though warm colours were used to make these suns, they look different because of where the centre is placed and how the rays are drawn?

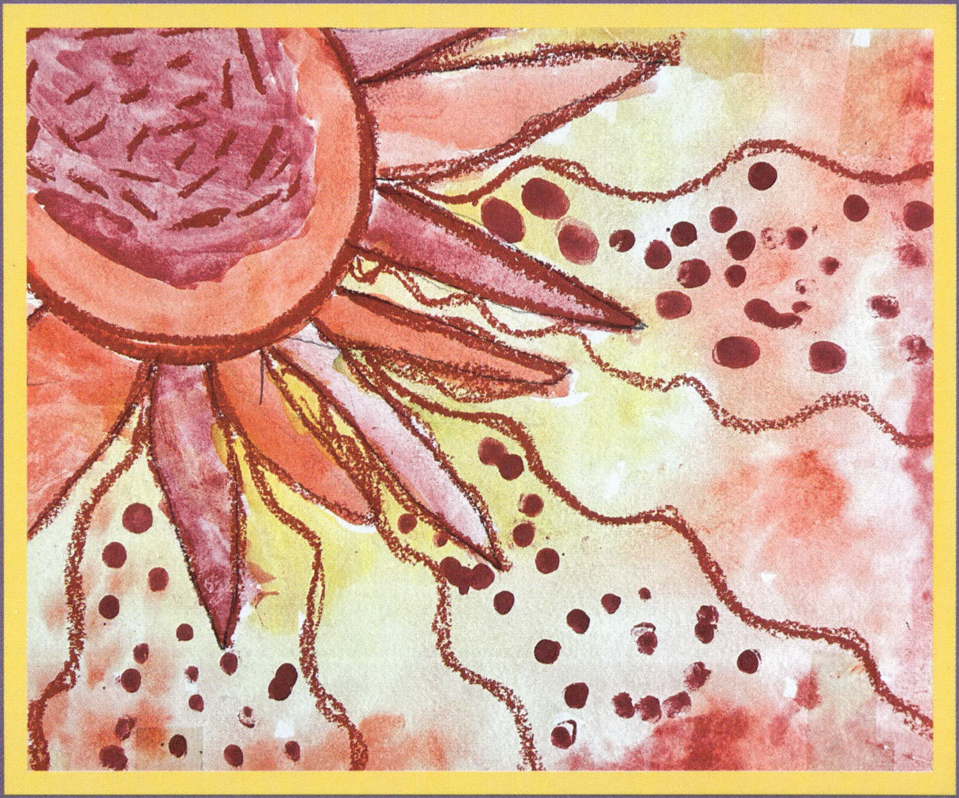

Now it's your turn to draw your own sun here and colour it using warm colours.

ART SUPPLIES: Oil pastels, watercolours, thick brush, bowl of water

Cool Colour Canvas

What do you notice about the colours of plants and water? When we look at forests, fields, rivers or even a nearby pond, we feel calm.

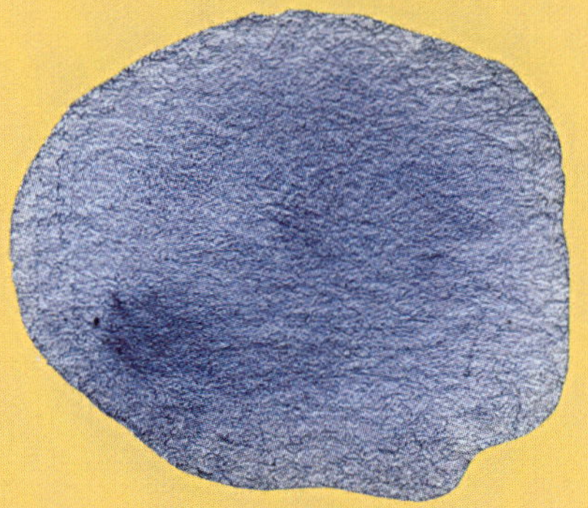

We see a lot of light and dark blues, purples and greens. These are called COOL COLOURS.

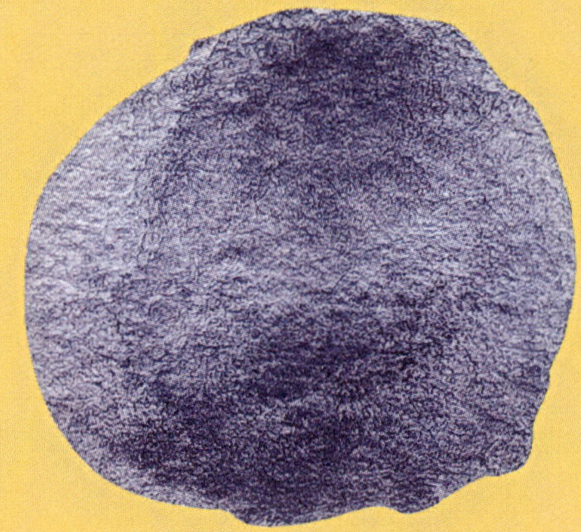

PRO TIP

If you don't have purple, you can make it! Mix a little red and a little blue. They come together to make purple!

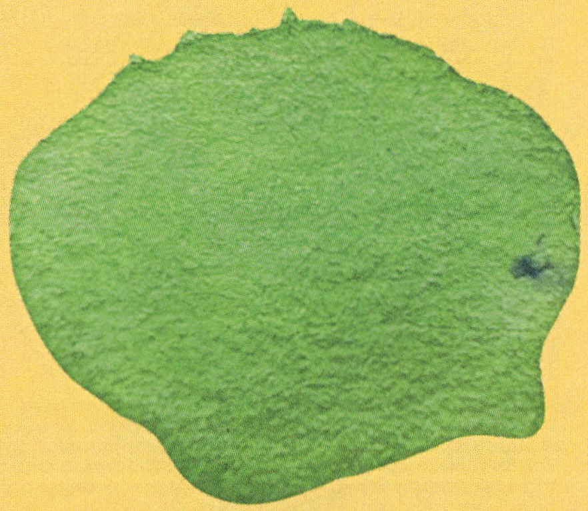

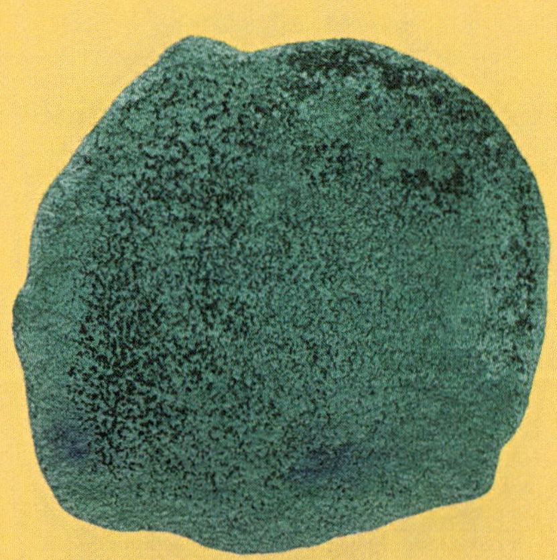

Let’s make some plants out of these patches of cool colours. It helps to look carefully at the shape and imagine what plant it could be. Here are some fun examples for you!

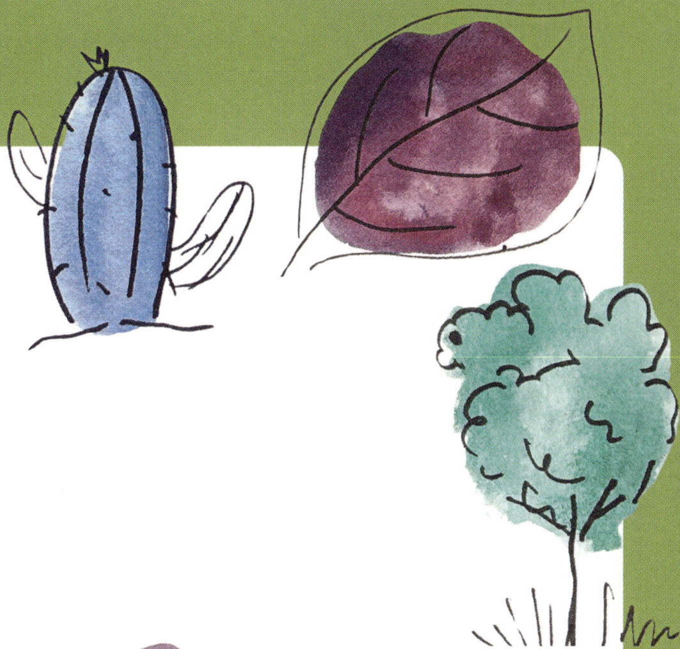

Let's look at the work of two artists who painted lily ponds. Do you see how in both paintings the artists have used cool colours?

Claude Monet lived in a beautiful small town called Giverny just outside of Paris. His garden was full of flowers, but his favourite part was the lily pond. He wanted his paintings to show how the water changed colours through the day.

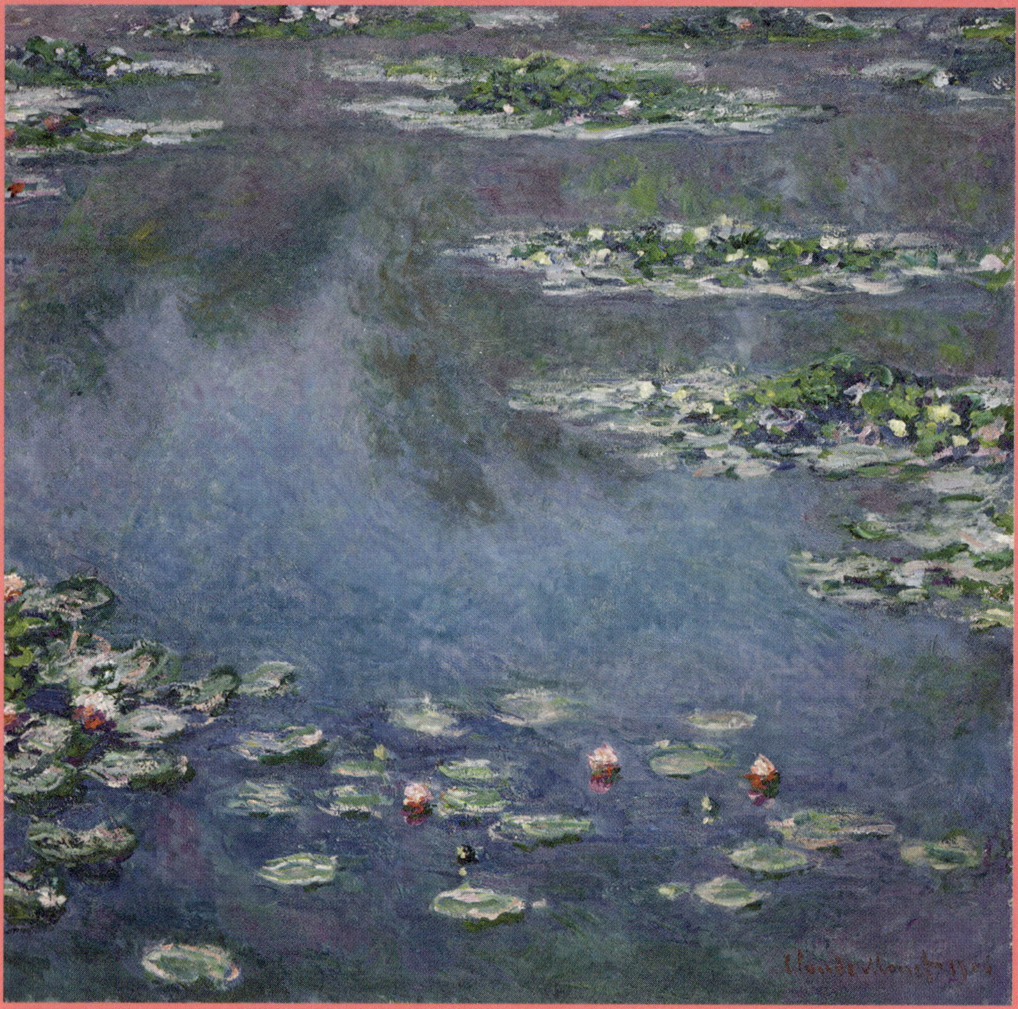

Artist: Claude Monet

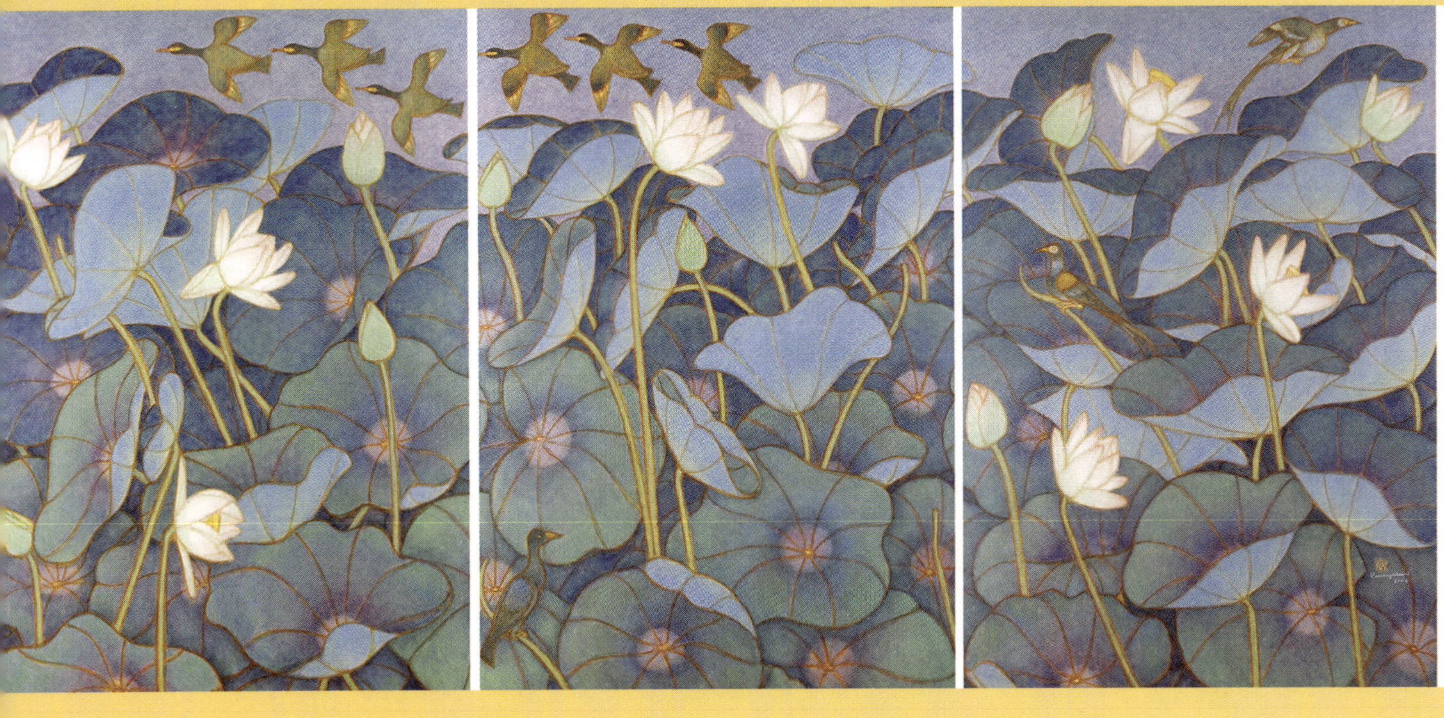

Artist: A. Ramachandran

A. Ramachandran grew up in a small village in Kerala surrounded by trees, fields and ponds. He became an artist and lived in Delhi, but he would travel to the countryside to think and paint. He especially liked to sit in a boat on a lotus pond with his sketchbook.

This painting of his is so full of leaves and flowers that we can't even see the water! But we know it's there.

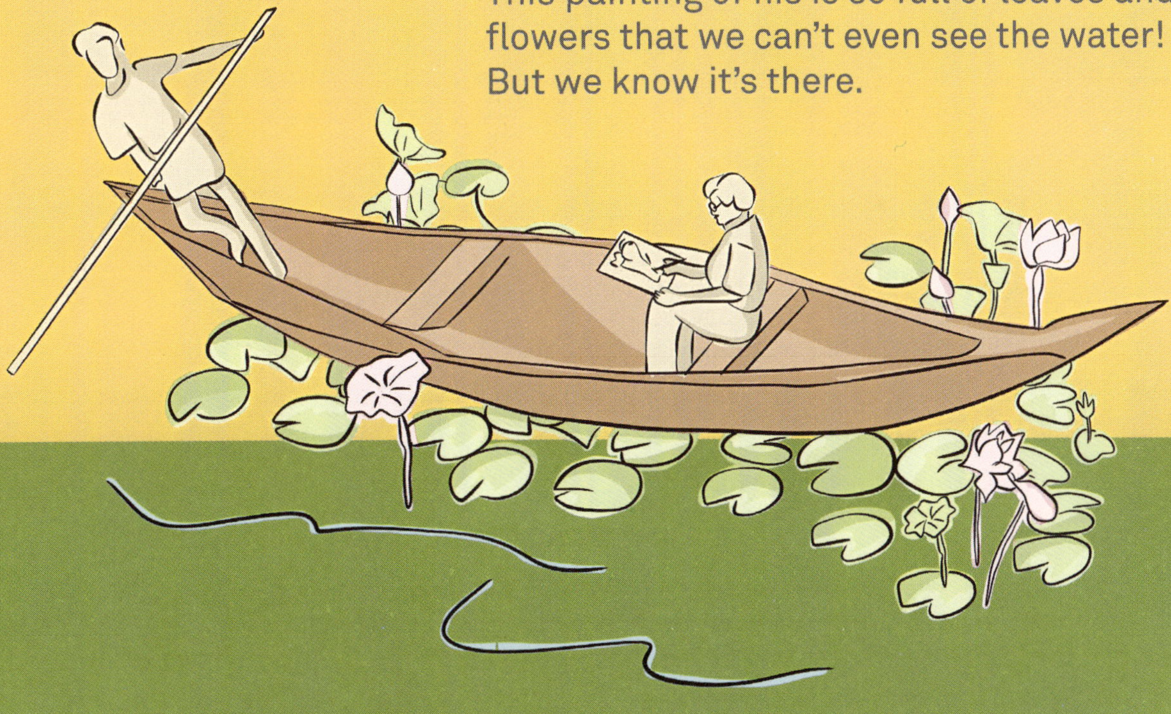

Tissue Paper Dabbing

Get ready to paint! You can choose any cool colours, and paint a small section on a blank paper. Remember the cool colours are green, blue and purple.

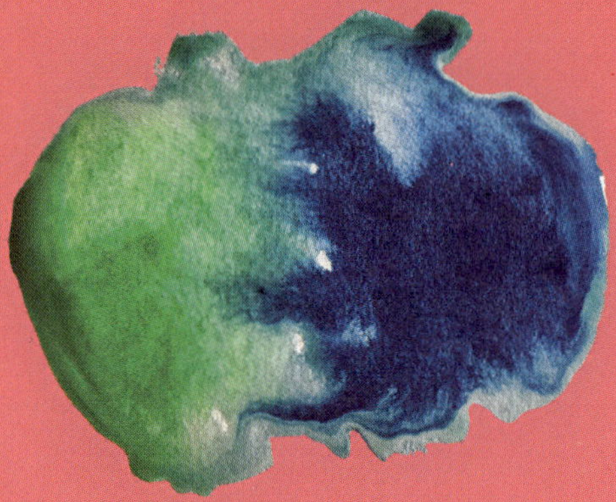

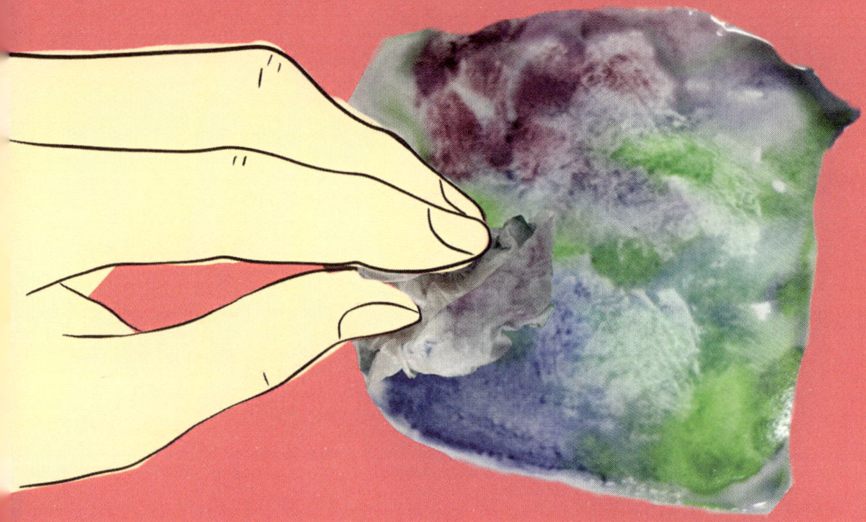

While the paint is still wet, dab a crumpled tissue on the wet paint. What do you see?

The tissue removes some of the water. This creates lighter colours.

Isn't that a fun trick ?

If you repeat this step using different cool colours, you can make a beautiful pond. It's ok to leave some white parts. They make the water look like it sparkles!

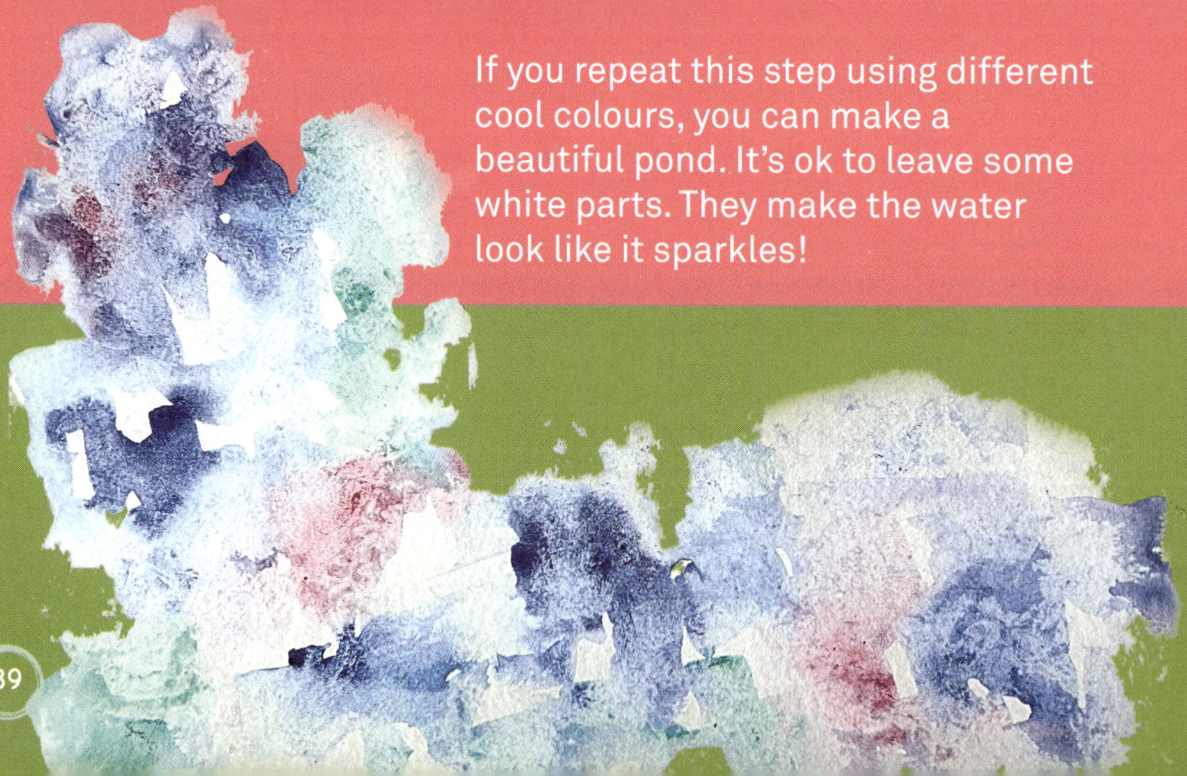

Colour the plants and animals with oil pastels. Once you're done, use watercolour paint to add cool colour patches, and dab using tissue paper to create your pond.

ART SUPPLIES: Oil pastels, watercolours, thick paint brush, bowl of water, tissue paper

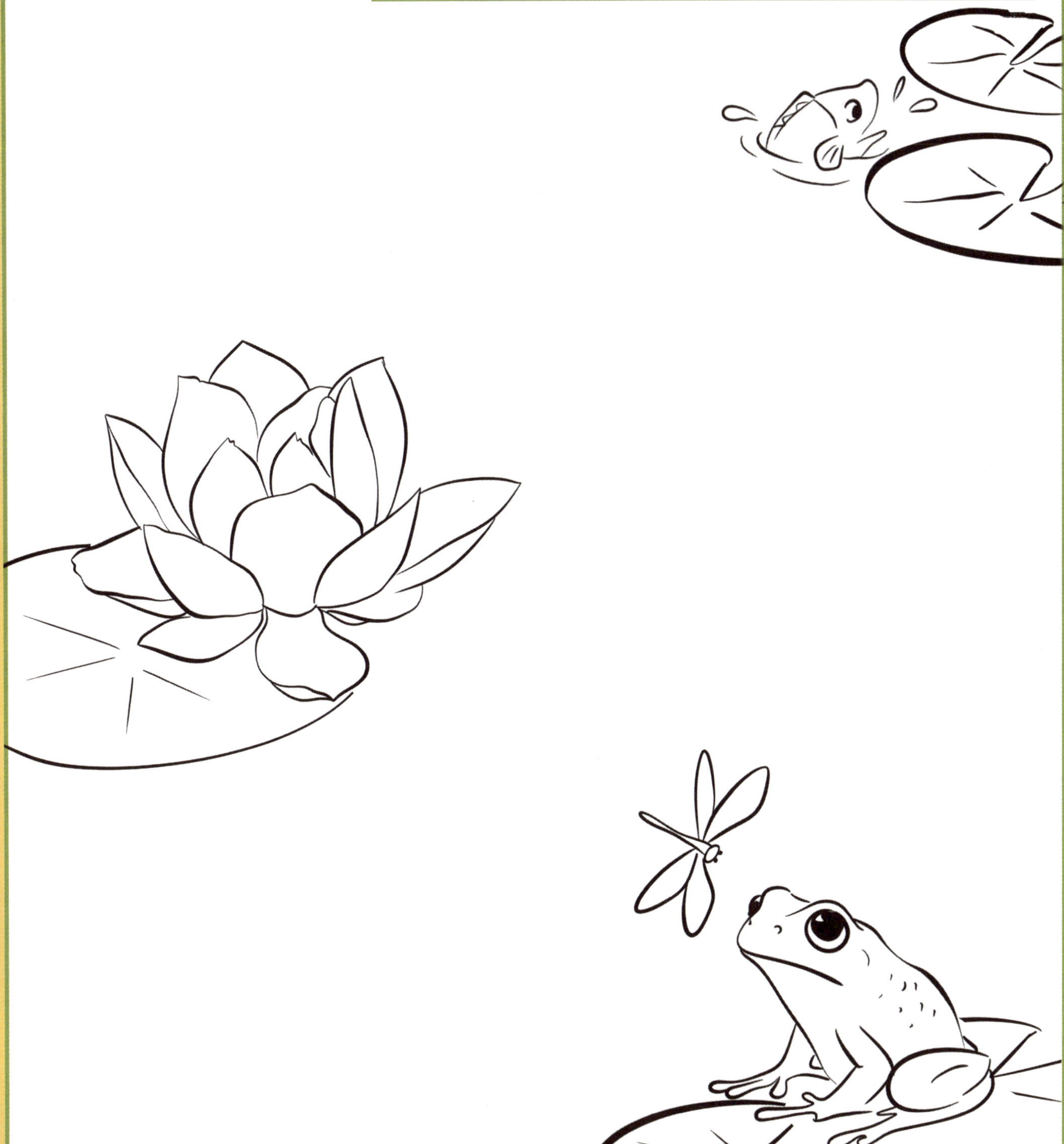

Loopy Pets

When we draw a line around a space, we create a SHAPE.

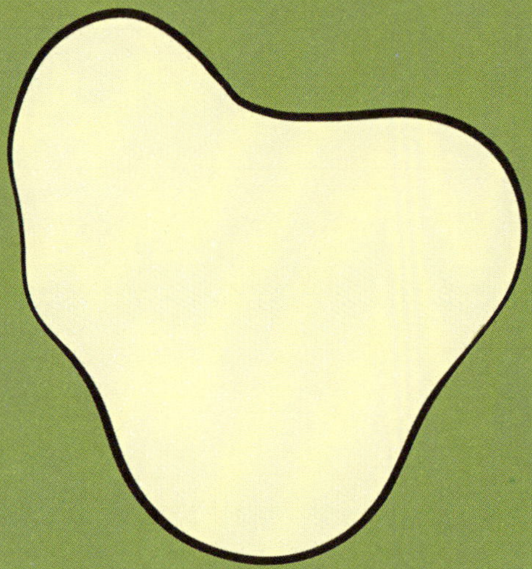

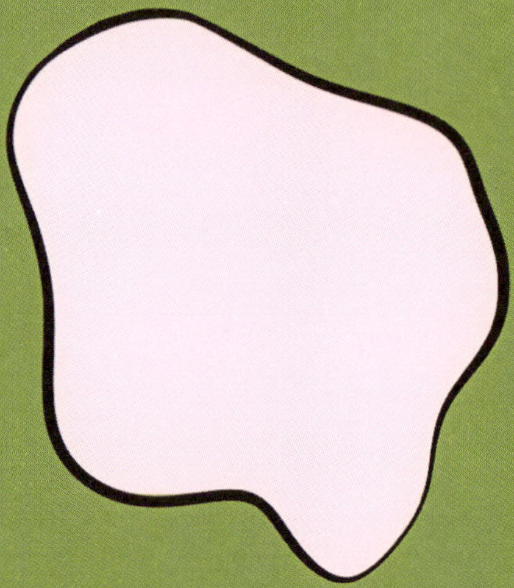

If you look carefully, you will see shapes everywhere—the shape of your hand, a leaf, or even a puddle.

Shapes can be building blocks when we want to draw anything.

Let's practice drawing some fun shapes.

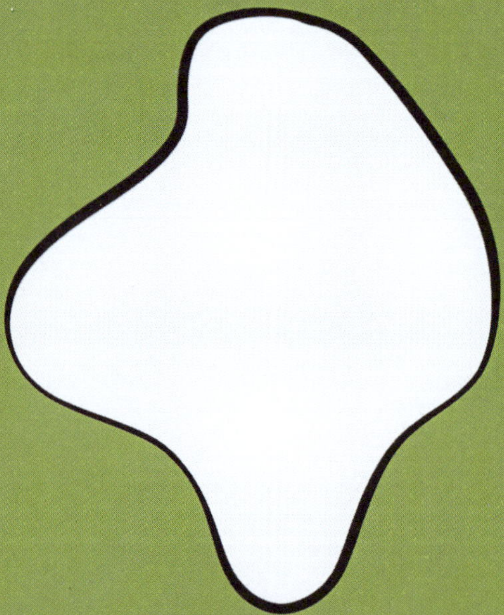

You can make a loopy pet by drawing a black wiggly, wavy line around the eyes and mouth. Maybe add special features like a hat, glasses, hands and feet.

ART SUPPLIES: Oil pastels

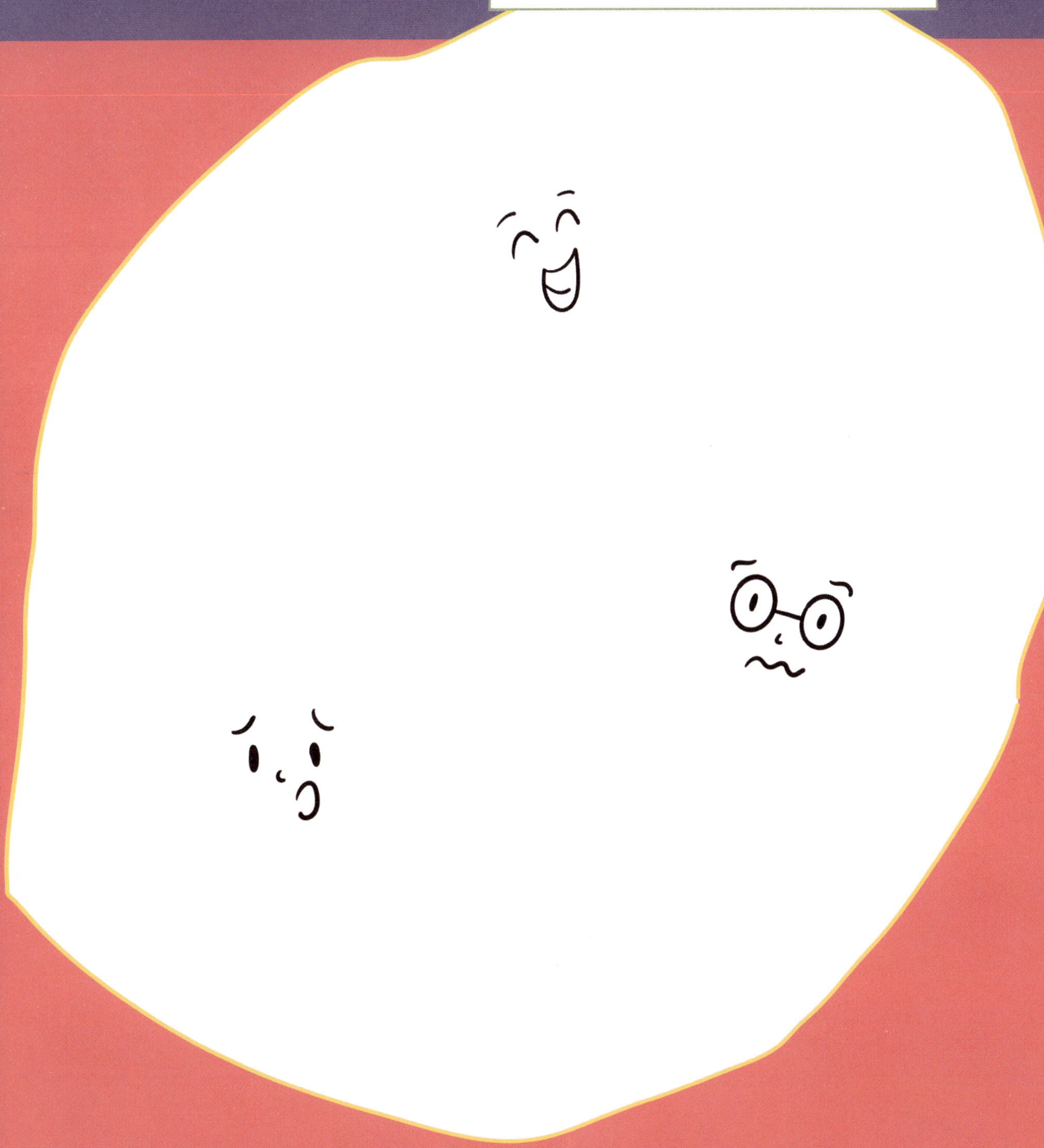

Shape Shortcut

Some common shapes are circle, oval, triangle, square and rectangle. If we draw a line down the middle of the shape, both sides look the same.

Can you complete the other half of these shapes? This is an art activity, so we won't use a ruler.

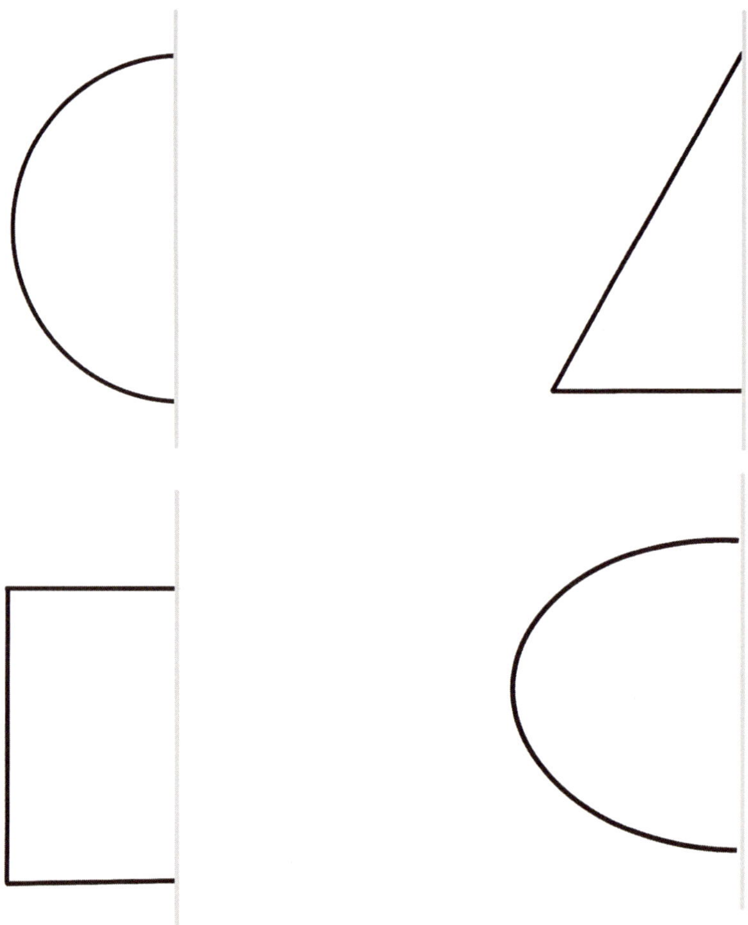

We can use shape shortcuts to help us draw anything!

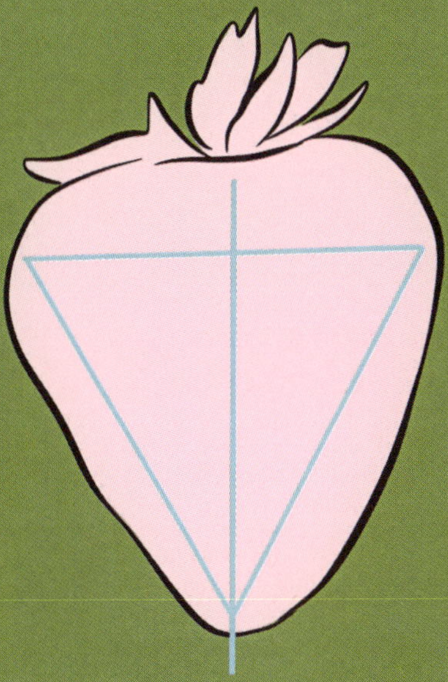

If you draw a line that curves around a triangle, and then draw leaves on top, you can make the shape of a strawberry

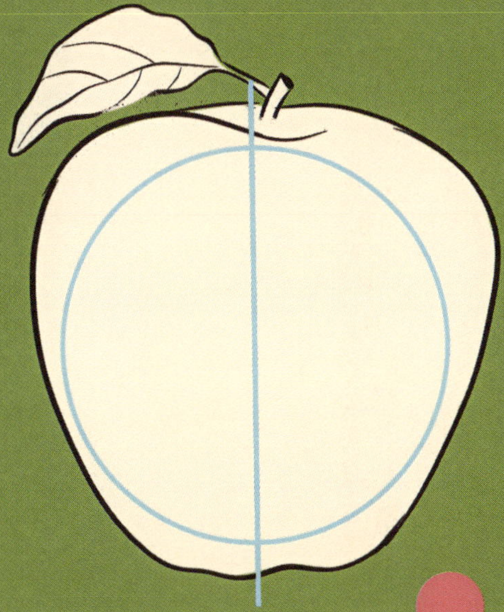

Notice how the outline of the apple looks like a circle with some extra curves.

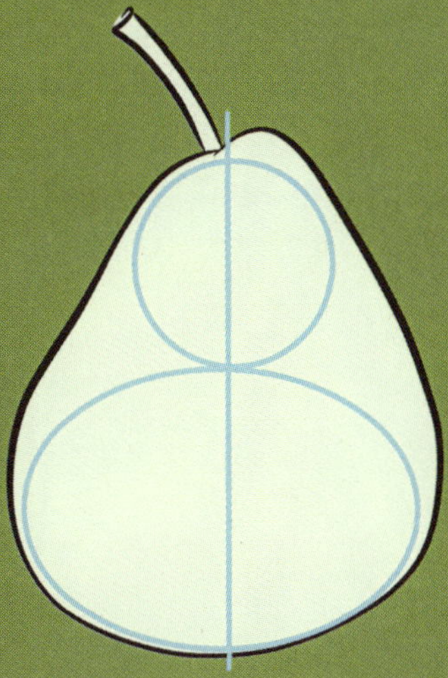

A pear shape is a bit trickier, but you can draw it by starting with a smaller circle on top of an oval.

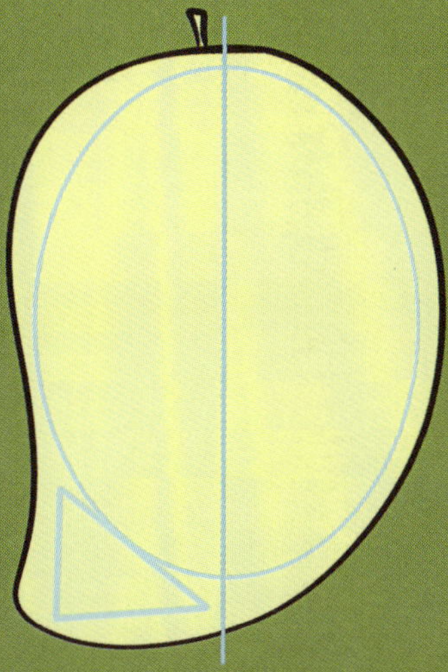

Mangoes have an interesting shape, an oval with a small tilted triangle at the bottom.

Oil Pastel Blending

1 Choose two oil pastel colours—the colour we see most in the fruit, and then a lighter or darker colour to make it look like the real thing.

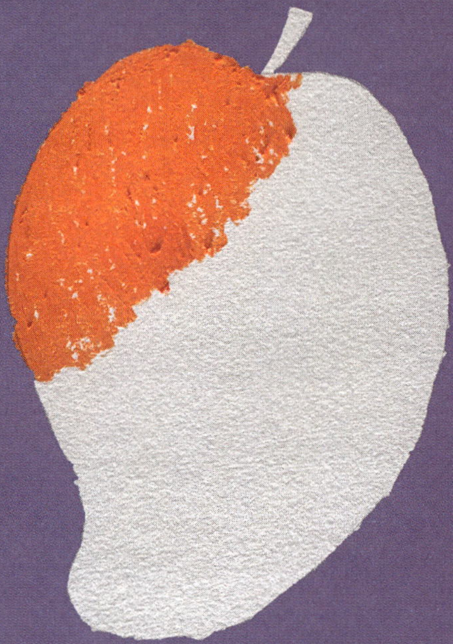

2 Hold the oil pastel like you would a pencil, and move it back and forth in one direction. Colour an area with one colour, then add another colour right next to it. Let the two colours mix up a little.

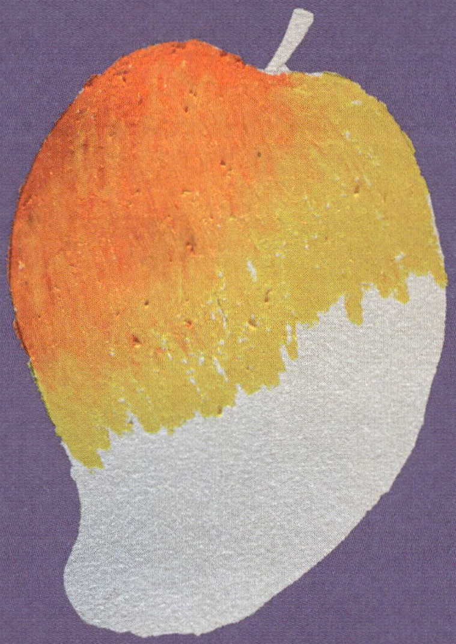

3 Where the two colours meet, try moving your hand in small circles until they mix together and make a new colour. That's a cool trick called BLENDING!

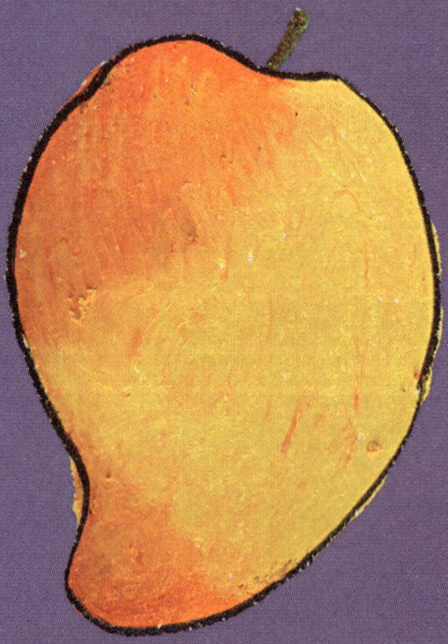

PRO TIP

Outline your work with a black oil pastel to see its shape more clearly.

Choose oil pastels in any two colours and practice blending here. Go ahead and have fun. Experiment to see which colours work best together.

ART SUPPLIES: Oil pastels

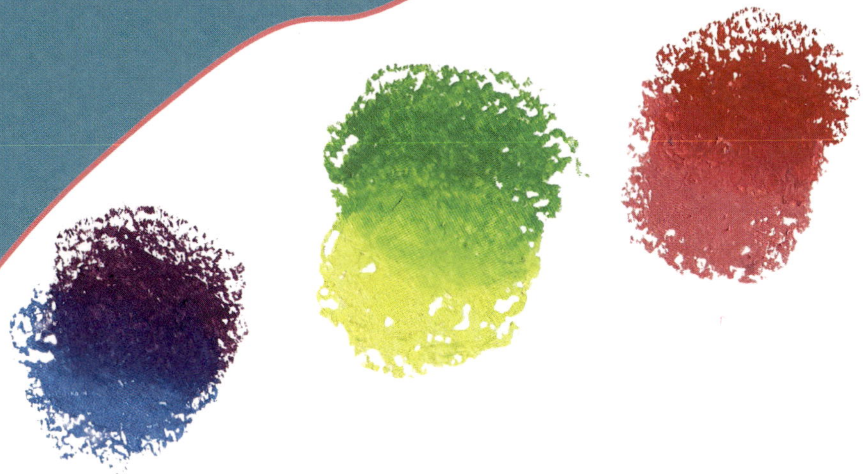

While apples may look red and pears may look green, if you look carefully, you can often find a second or even a third colour.

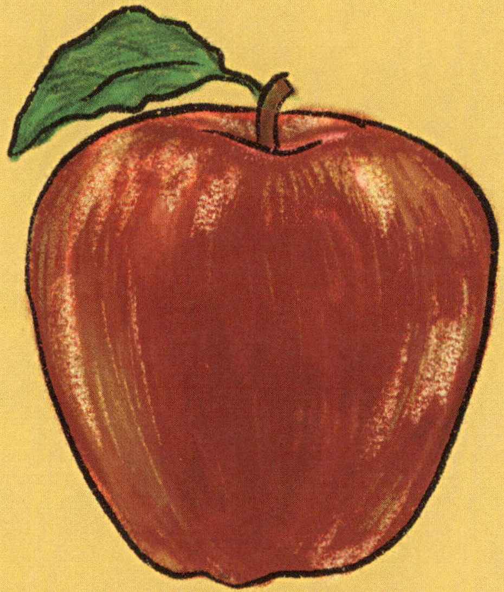

How to decide what colours to blend with? See how some parts of the apple are lighter? We can use yellow on the top and at the sides to show the lighter parts.

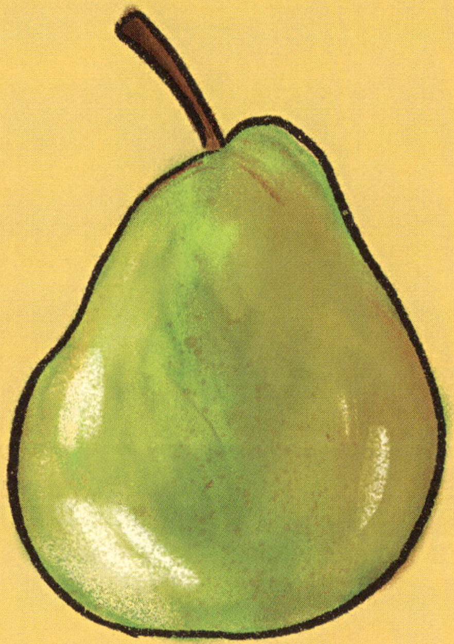

Look carefully at your pear—which part is lighter? Again, we can use yellow or white for the lighter parts, and dark green or red for the darker parts.

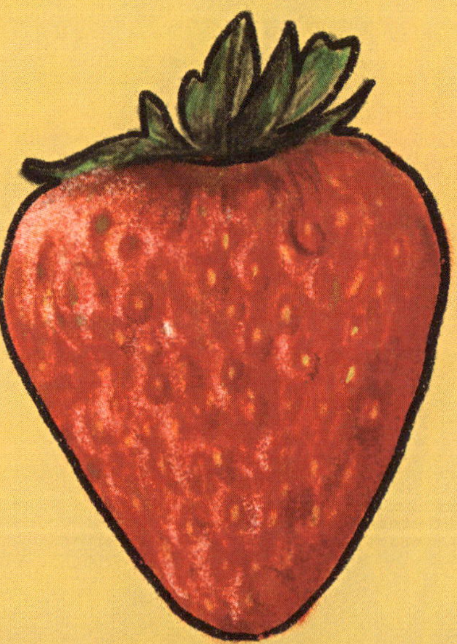

When we colour the strawberry, we can also use some brown for the darker parts.

If you outline your fruit with a black oil pastel, it will stand out from the background.

Are you ready? Choose a fruit you like and look carefully at it. Draw it using the shape shortcut. Next, use the oil pastel blending method to colour it, and don't forget to outline it with black oil pastel.

ART SUPPLIES: Oil pastels

Drawing Tools

We learned how to draw fruits using the shape shortcut. Now let's look at how we can use it to draw something with many parts.
Tools help us to do our work more easily. Can you name some tools?

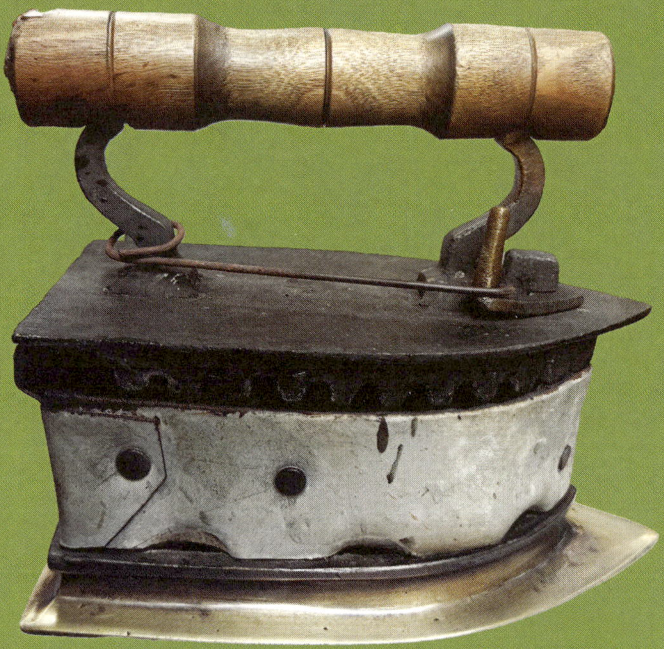

Have you seen a man on the street using a coal iron to press wrinkles out of clothes?

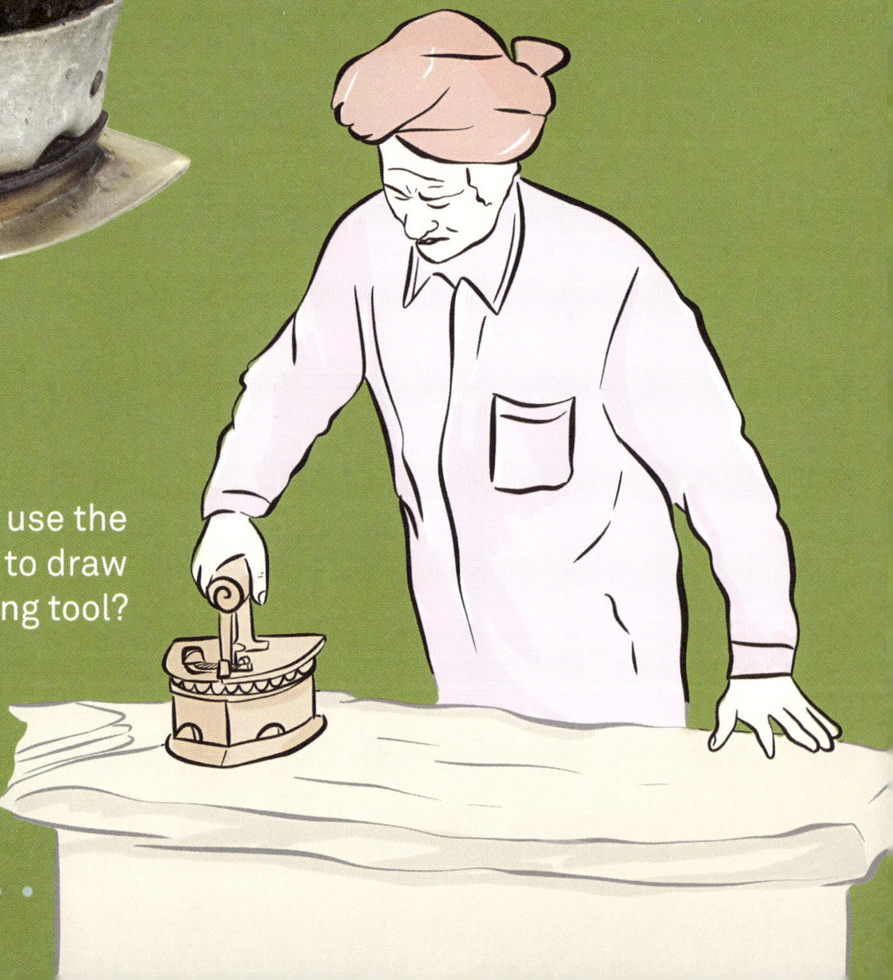

How would you use the shape shortcut to draw this interesting tool?

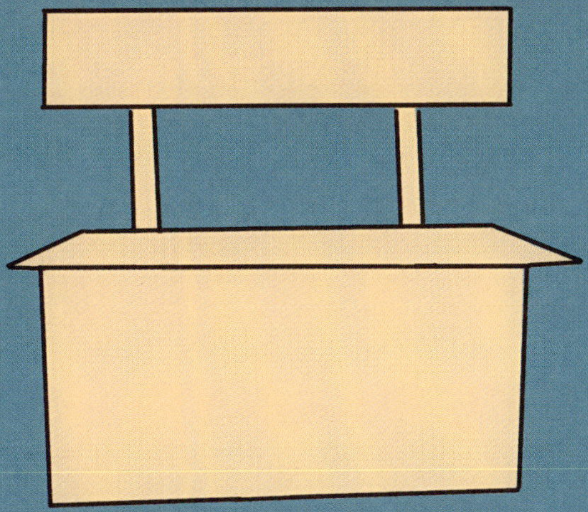

First, draw the big rectangle and a long thin rectangle above it, with some smaller shapes joining them.

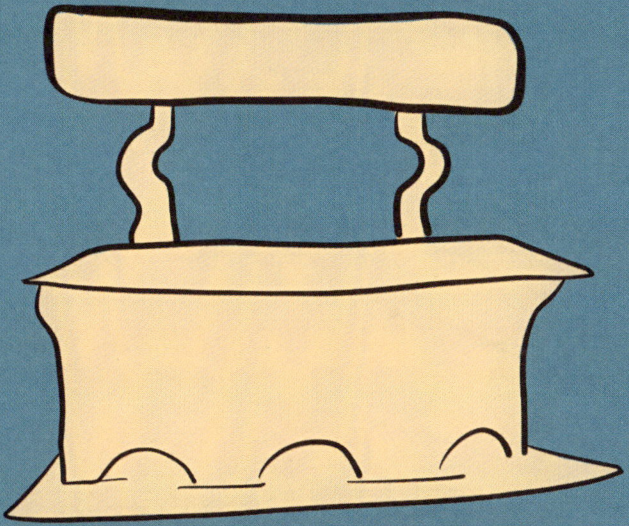

Next, we can draw the flat metal plate under it, and the three small curves. What other details can you spot?

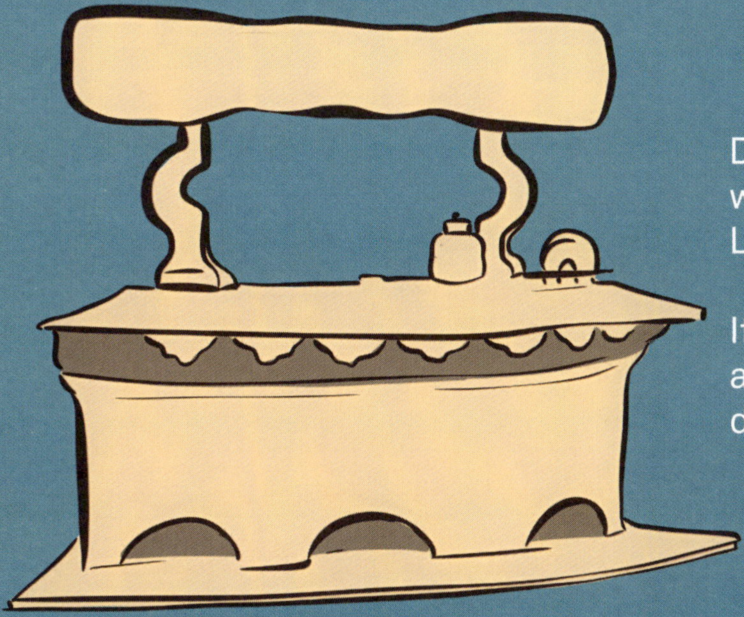

Do you notice that some parts which have gaps look dark? Let's fill them in.

If you just look for the shapes and go step-by-step, you can draw anything.

Sameer Kulavoor is an artist who made beautiful drawings of simple tools.

He lives in Mumbai. His big, crowded city has become a lot busier since the days when he would walk to school through paddy fields.

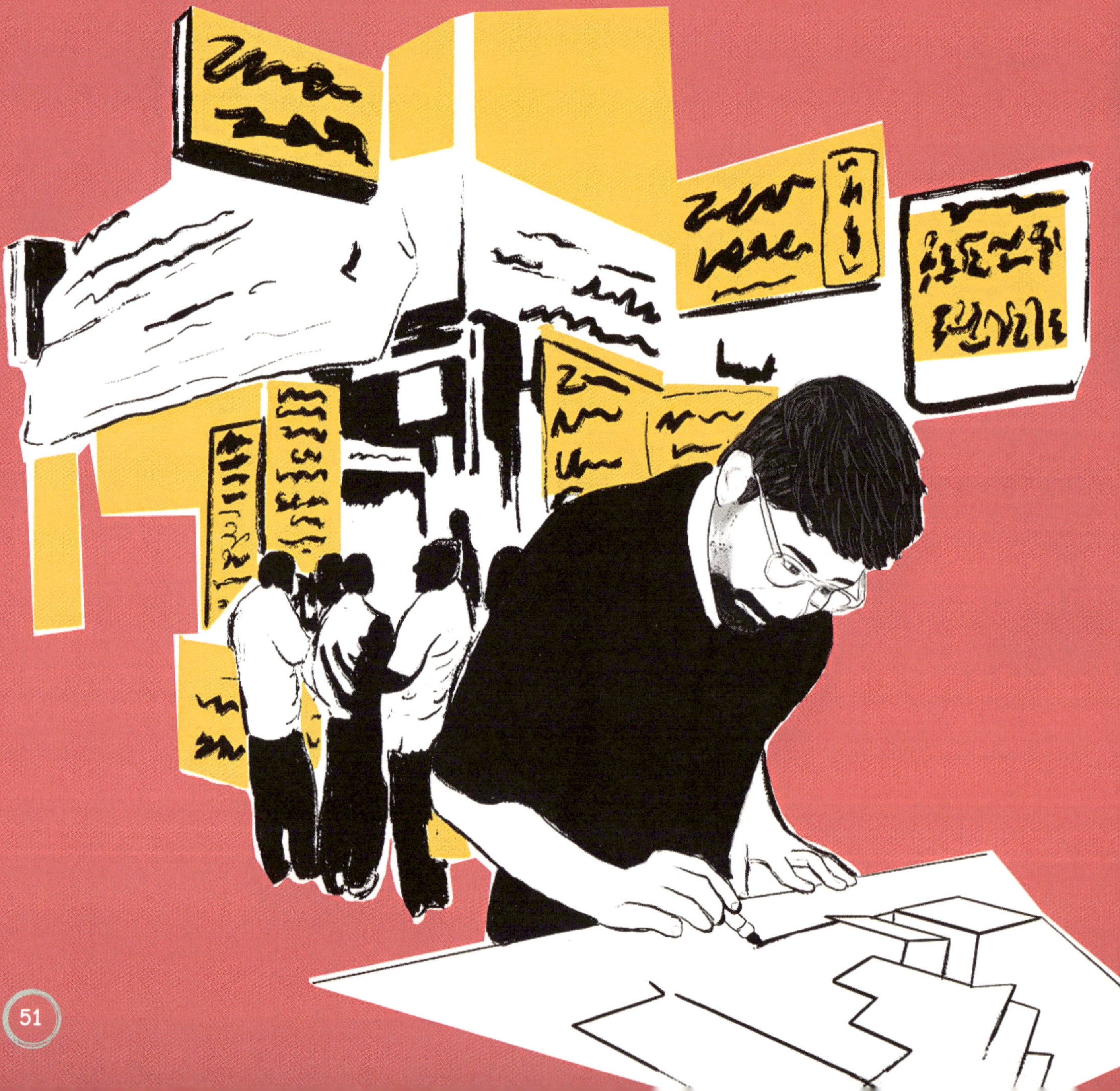

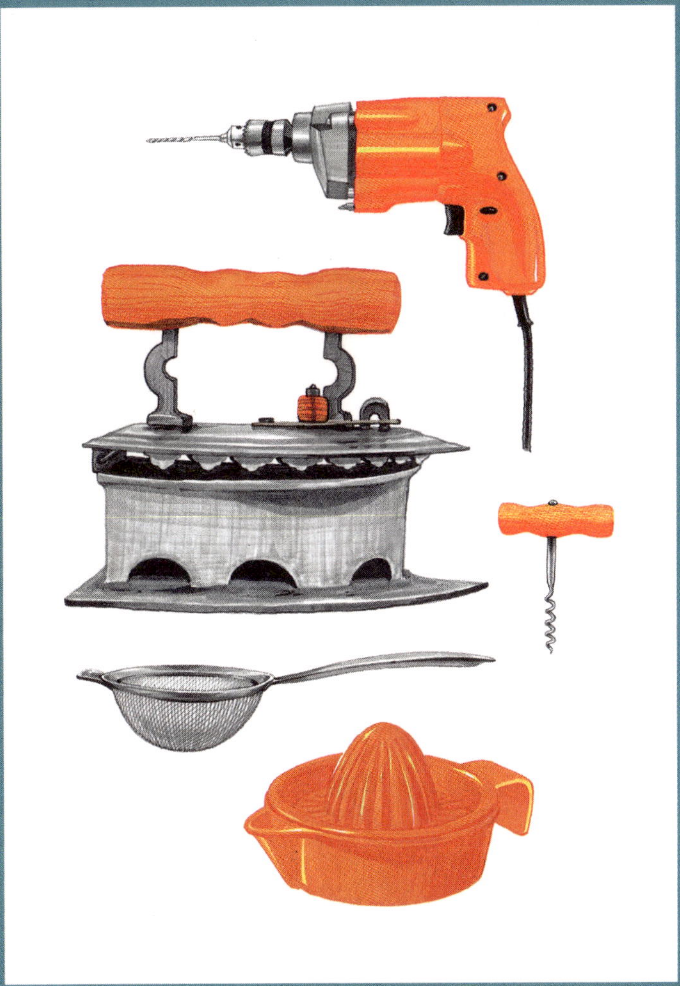

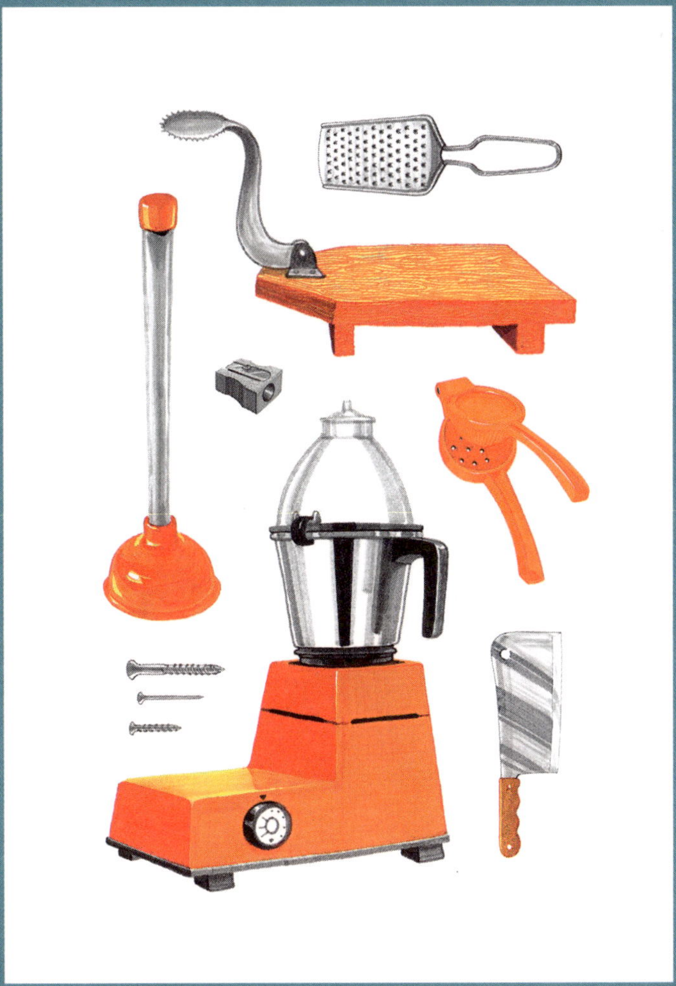

He drew these tools because when he's in Mumbai, he often feels tired, as if he were a fruit in a mixer being blended into juice, or being ironed out as if he were a shirt ...

Artist: Sameer Kulavoor

That's a new way to think about how we feel, isn't it?

Can you find a special tool in your home or neighbourhood? Write what the tool does and why you chose it.

Carefully look at the shape of the tool. Use the shape shortcut to draw the tool you chose.

ART SUPPLIES: Pencil, eraser, black sketch pen

Cat City

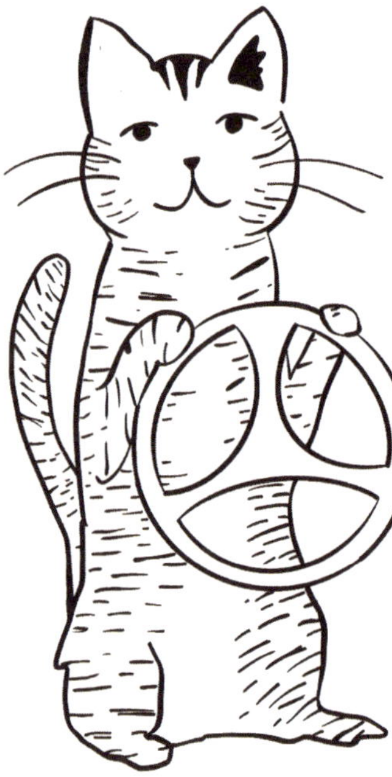

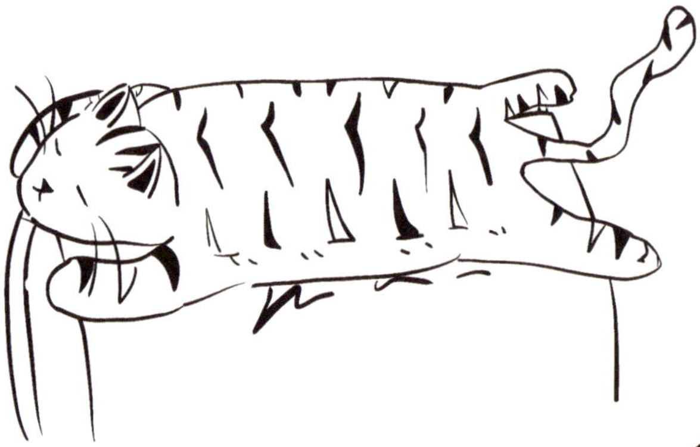

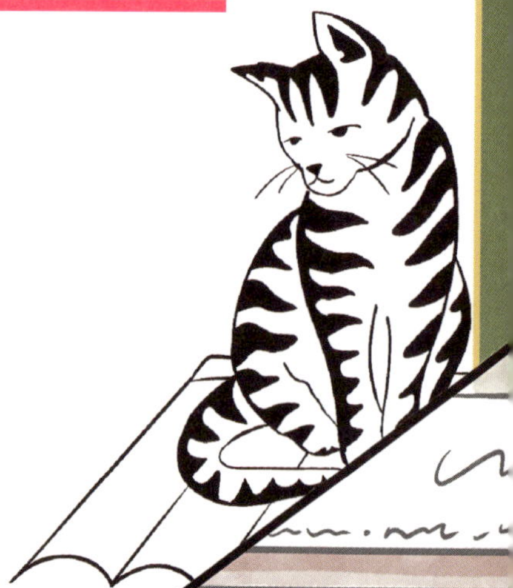

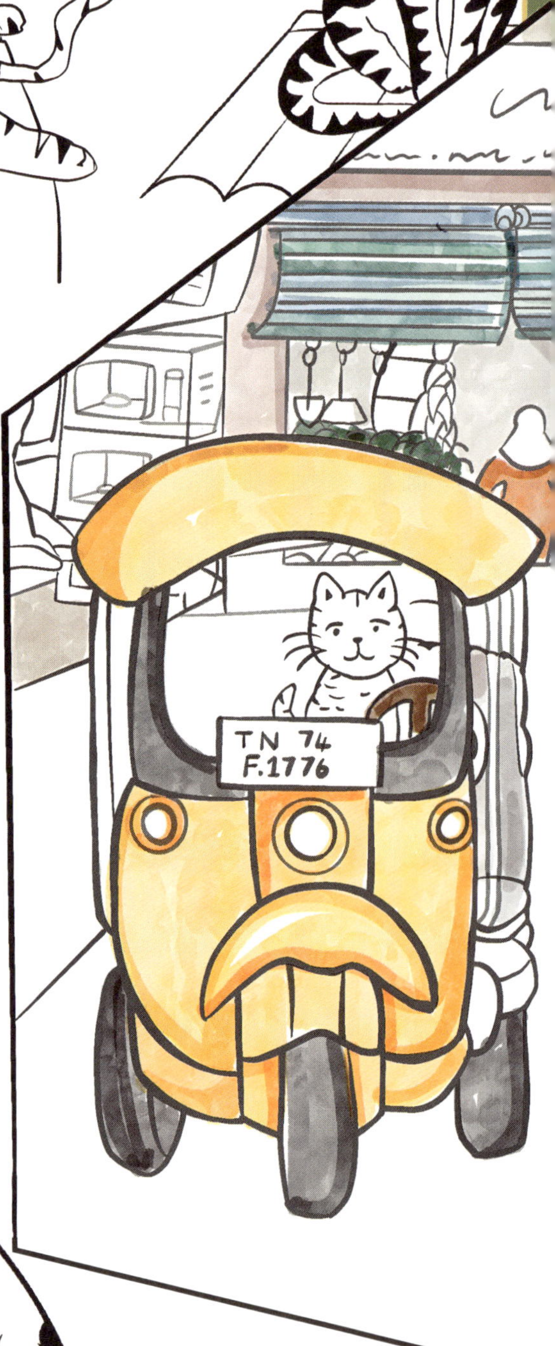

The cats we see are grey, black, white, brown or orange. Since we are artists, let's colour the cats using colours that are NOT cat colours.

Was that fun? Can you find these five cats in the picture?

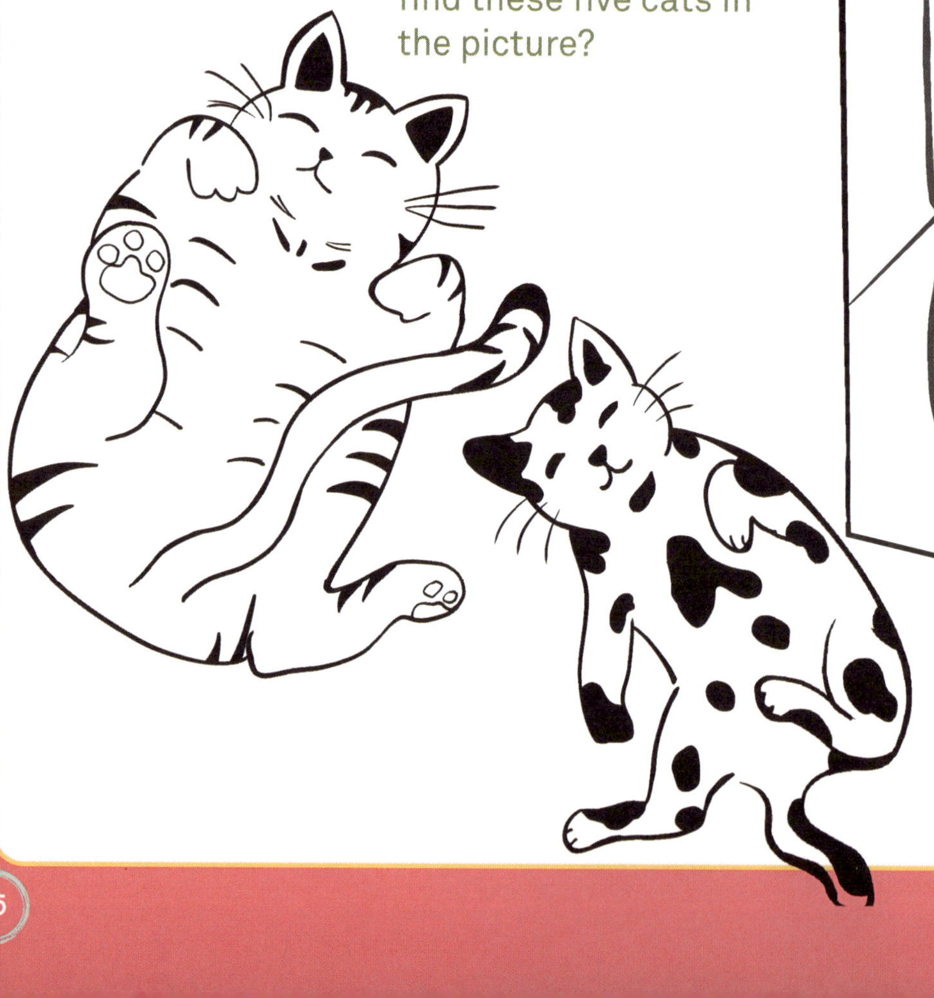

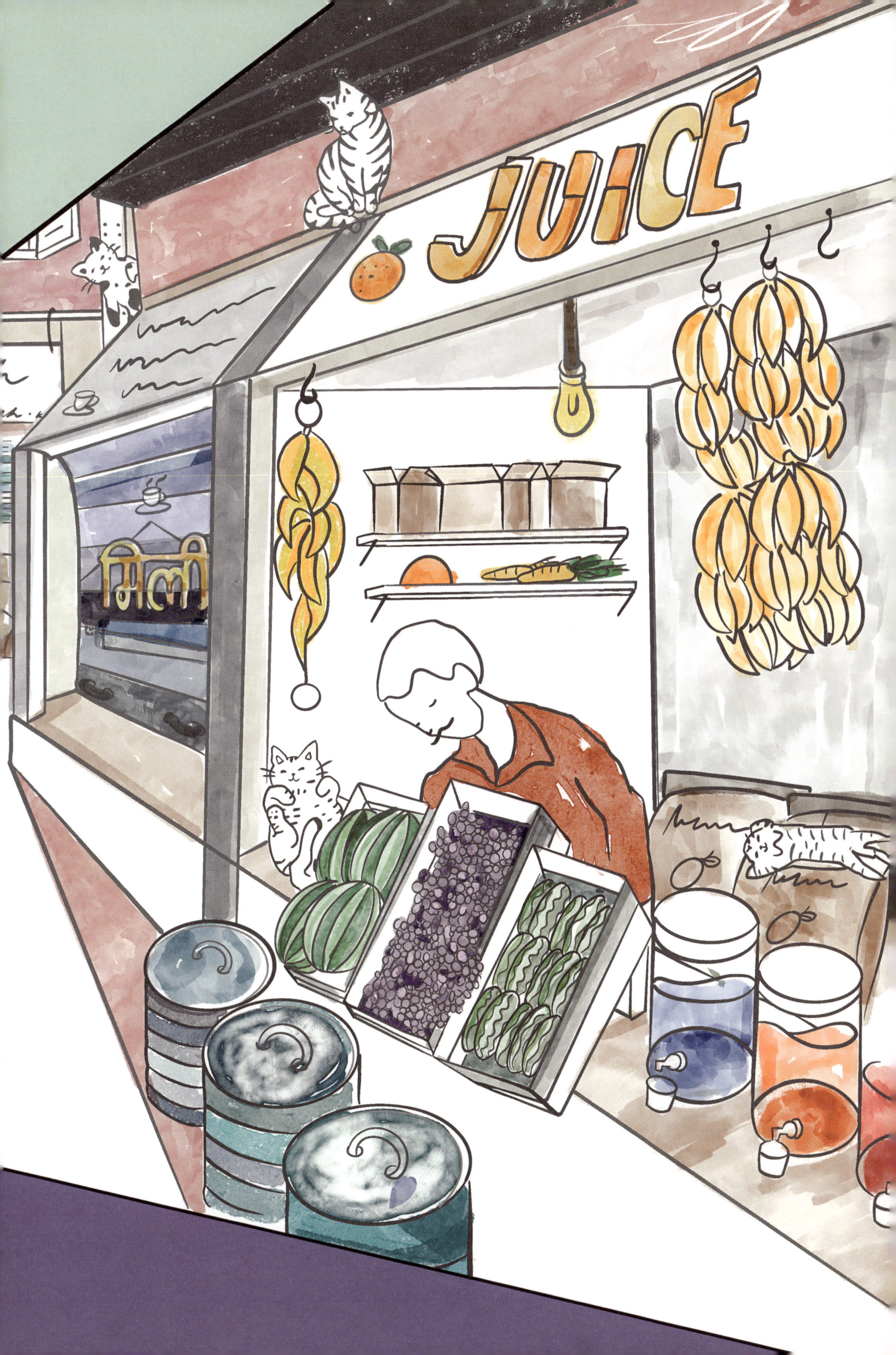
JUICE
मिली

This is My Face

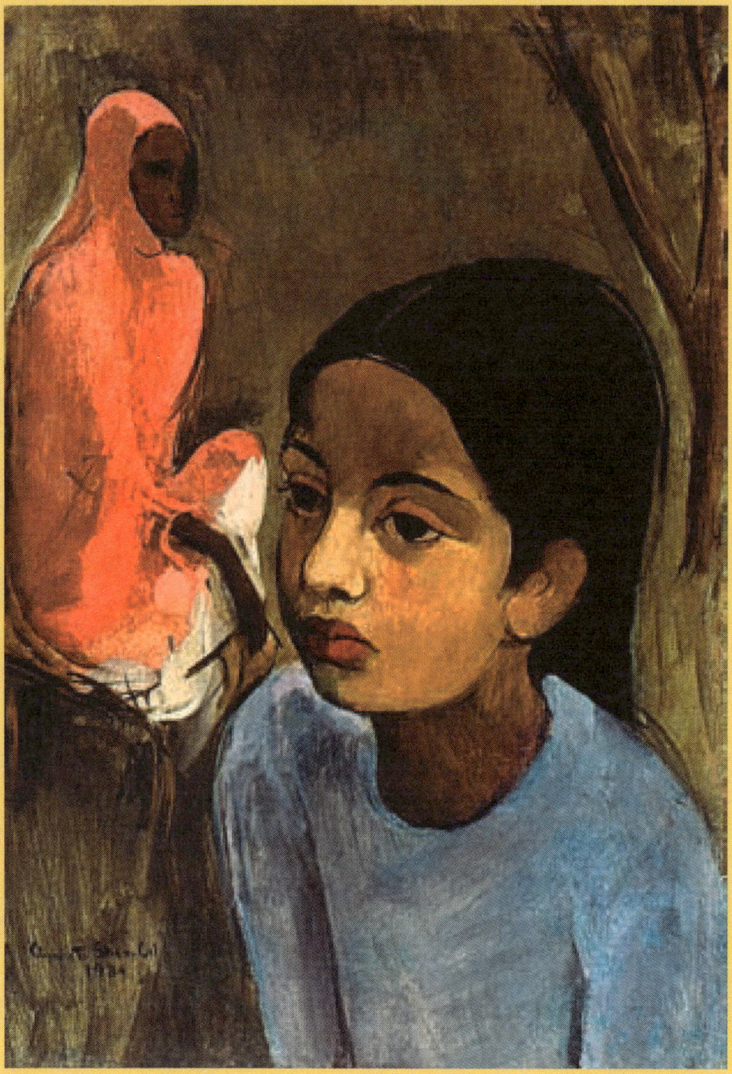

Artist: Amrita Sher-Gil

Many artists all over the world have drawn portraits. A PORTRAIT is a picture of someone's face.

Here is a portrait made by the Hungarian-Indian artist **Amrita Sher-Gil**. As a little girl, she loved painting faces. She would ask her family, friends and even people who worked in the house to pose for her drawings.

This is a painting of her eight year old neighbour.
What could she be thinking?
What do you notice in the background?

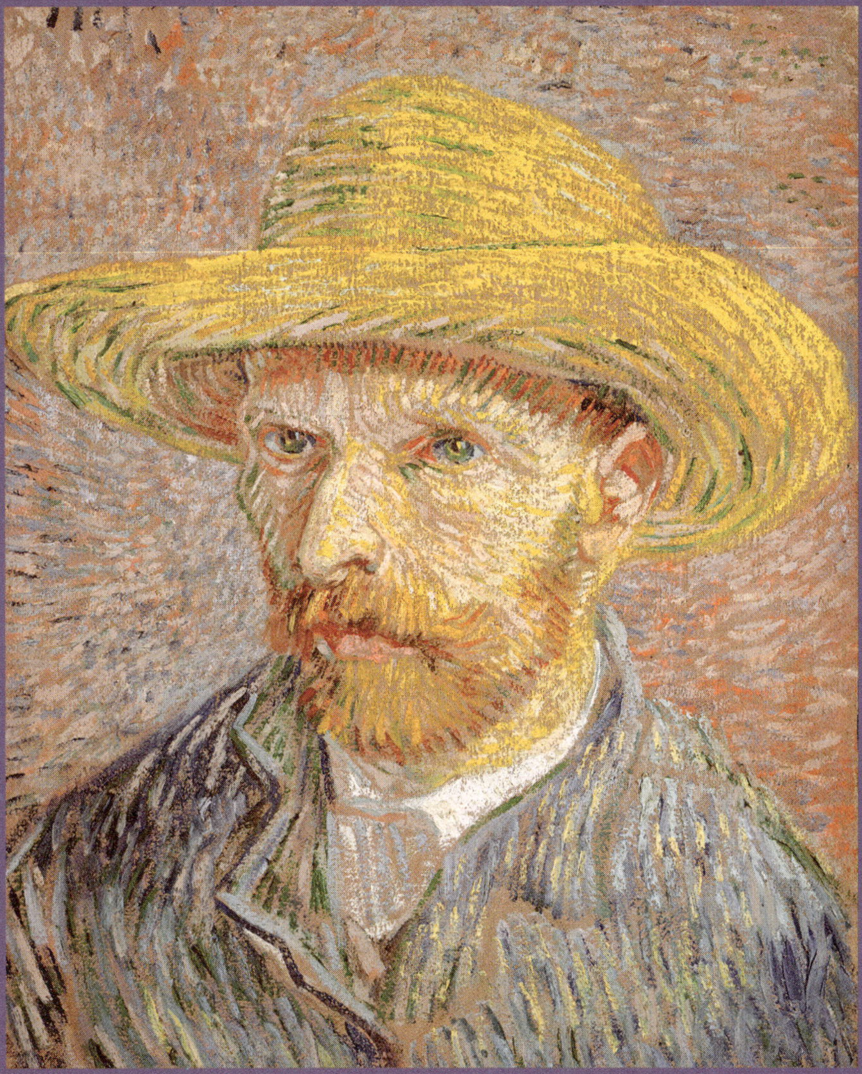

Artist: Vincent Van Gogh

When we draw our own face, it's called a SELF-PORTRAIT.

Vincent Van Gogh was a Dutch artist who loved to paint portraits. He made more than 35 self-portraits. That's a lot!

His self portraits became like a drawing diary for him. He would think about how he was feeling and then try to paint his mood.

Are you ready to make your own portrait?
Look carefully at your face in a small mirror.

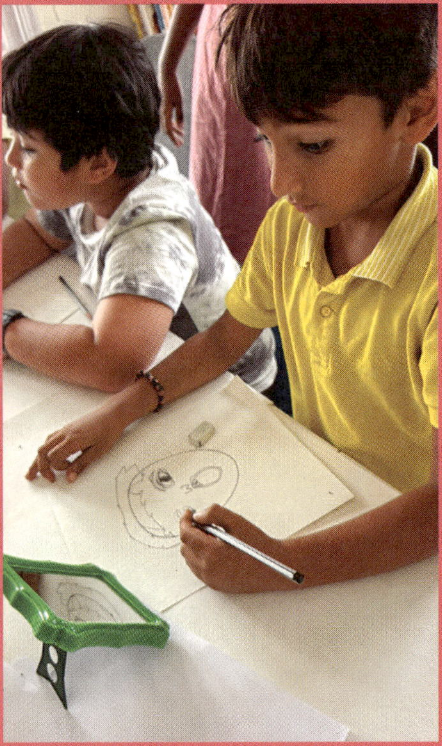

You can start by drawing your eyes. Our eyes are usually almond shaped. Notice the shape of your unique eyes. Are your eyebrows thick or thin?

Look carefully in the mirror again. How much of your hair do you see on your forehead? Does it cover your ears?

Let's make the background more exciting by adding simple line or shape patterns.

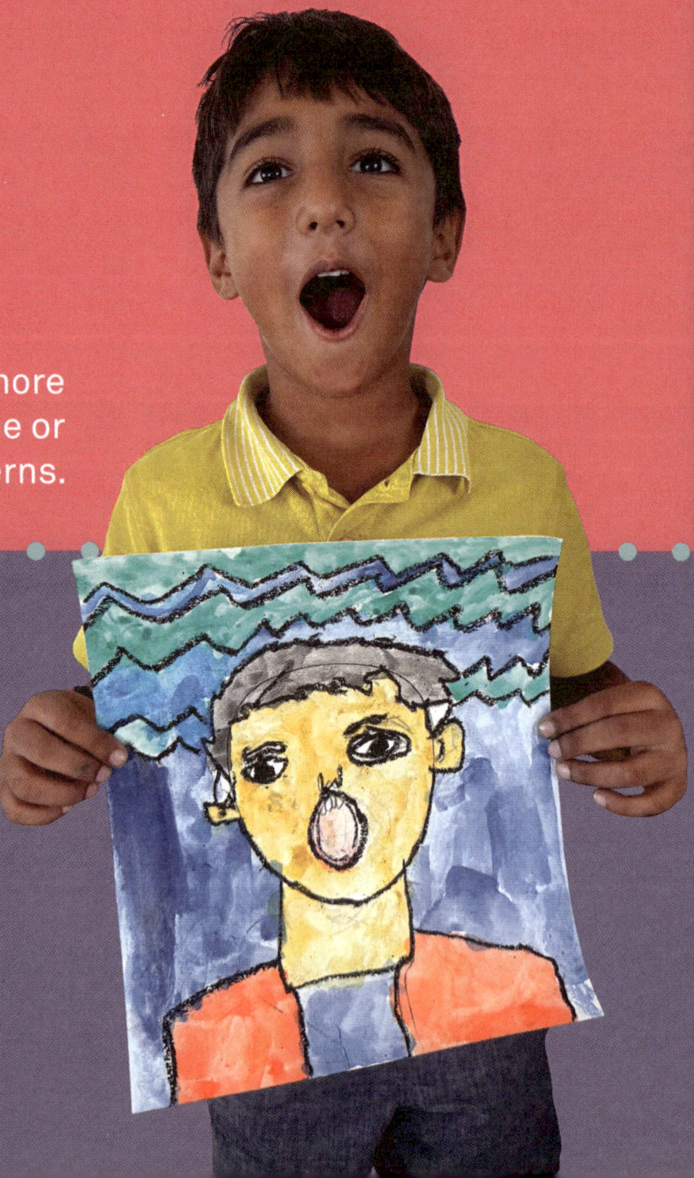

When we smile, the corners of our lips curve upwards. When you are surprised, your mouth almost forms a circle. When drawing your nose or your teeth, it's better to keep it simple and draw just a line or two.

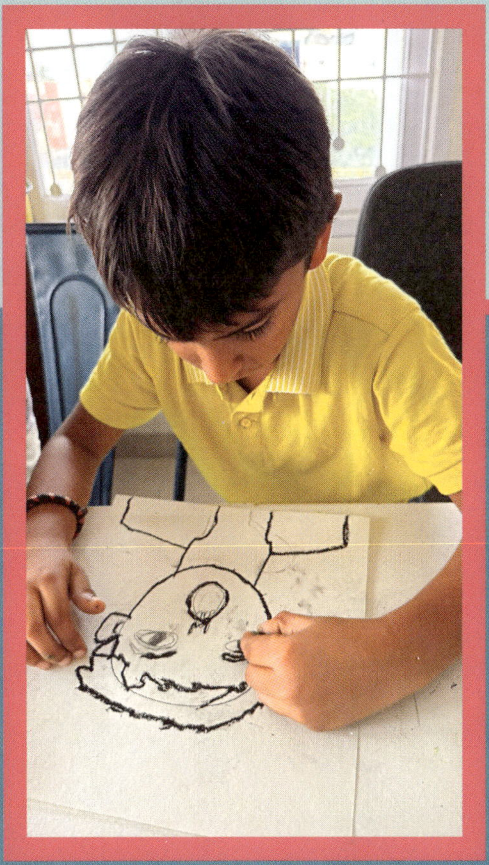

Use a black oil pastel to outline the picture.

You can use an oil pastel to colour any small parts that may be too tricky to paint with a brush, like your eyeball, hair and patterns on your clothes.

When colouring your hair with the oil pastel try making quick lines instead of colouring like a block.

For the larger areas, we will use watercolour paint.

Carefully paint the face and neck with a shade of yellow or brown that matches your skin. Is your hair black, brown or another colour? You can paint your hair colour too.

Try not to get any colour on the white parts of the face, like the eyes or teeth.

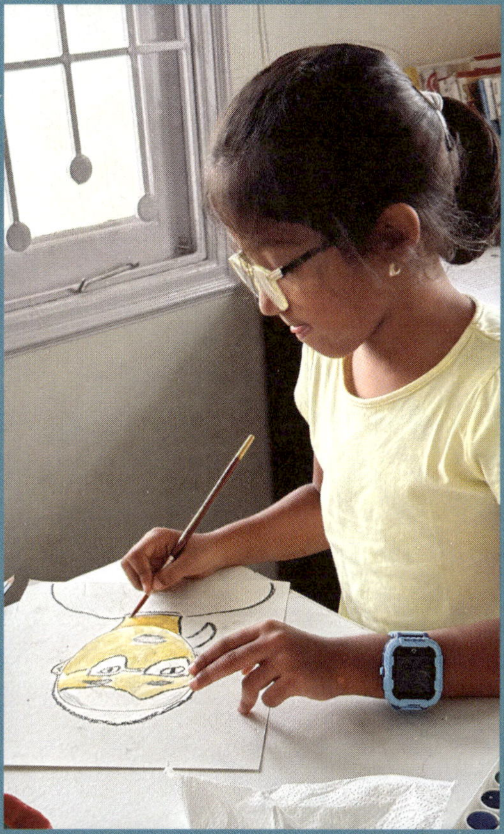

You can paint the background using colours that are different from your shirt, so that your portrait stands out against the background.

Like Van Gogh, you can create many self portraits to show your mood too!

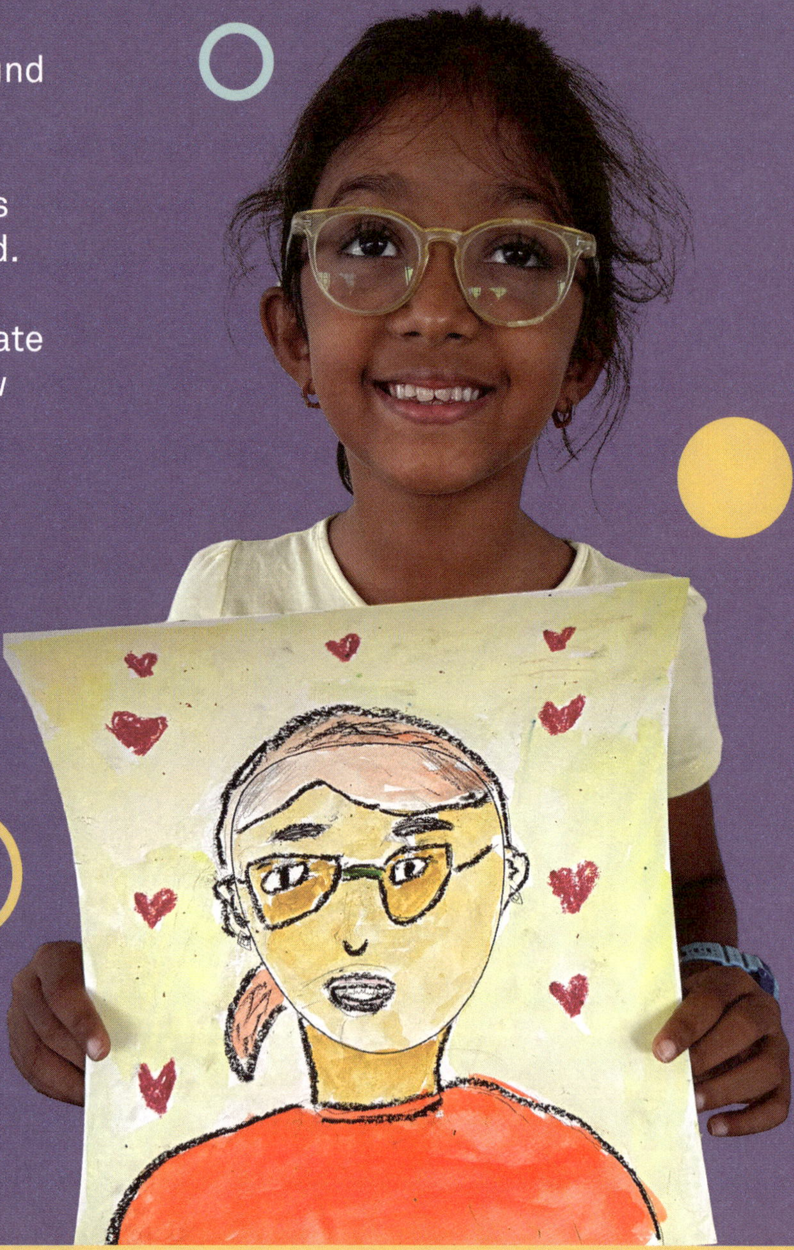

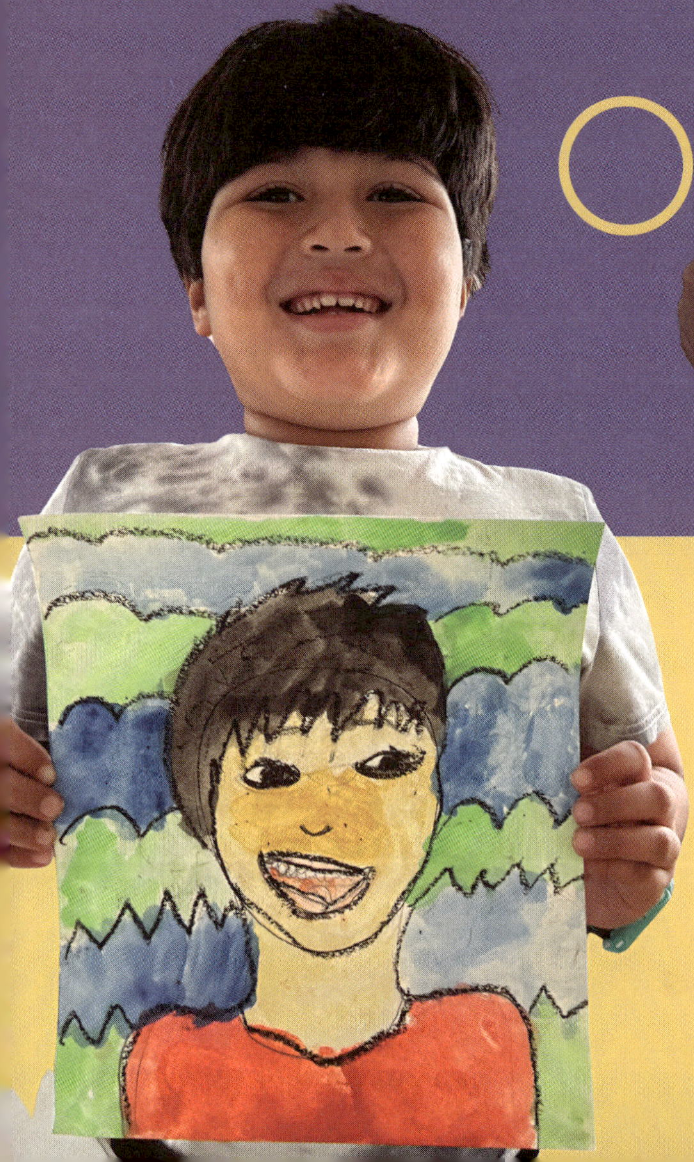

Hold your self-portrait next to you, and look in the mirror. Do you see how your self-portrait looks just like you?

Now it's your turn. Don't forget to keep looking in the mirror. You can use this shape as a starting point.

ART SUPPLIES: Oil pastels, watercolours, paint brush, bowl of water

Lion's Mane Collage

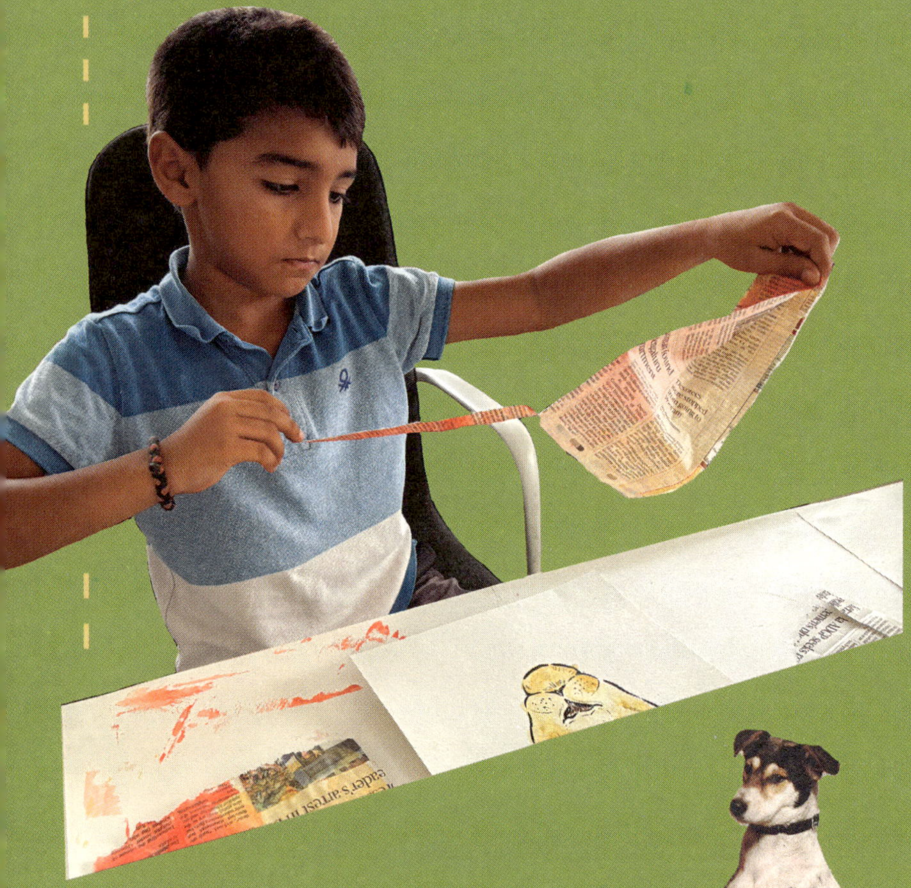

An interesting way to fill an artwork is by tearing and sticking paper. This is called a COLLAGE.

There are many ways to collect coloured papers to use in our collage. We can cut or tear pictures from old magazines, newspapers or use painted paper.

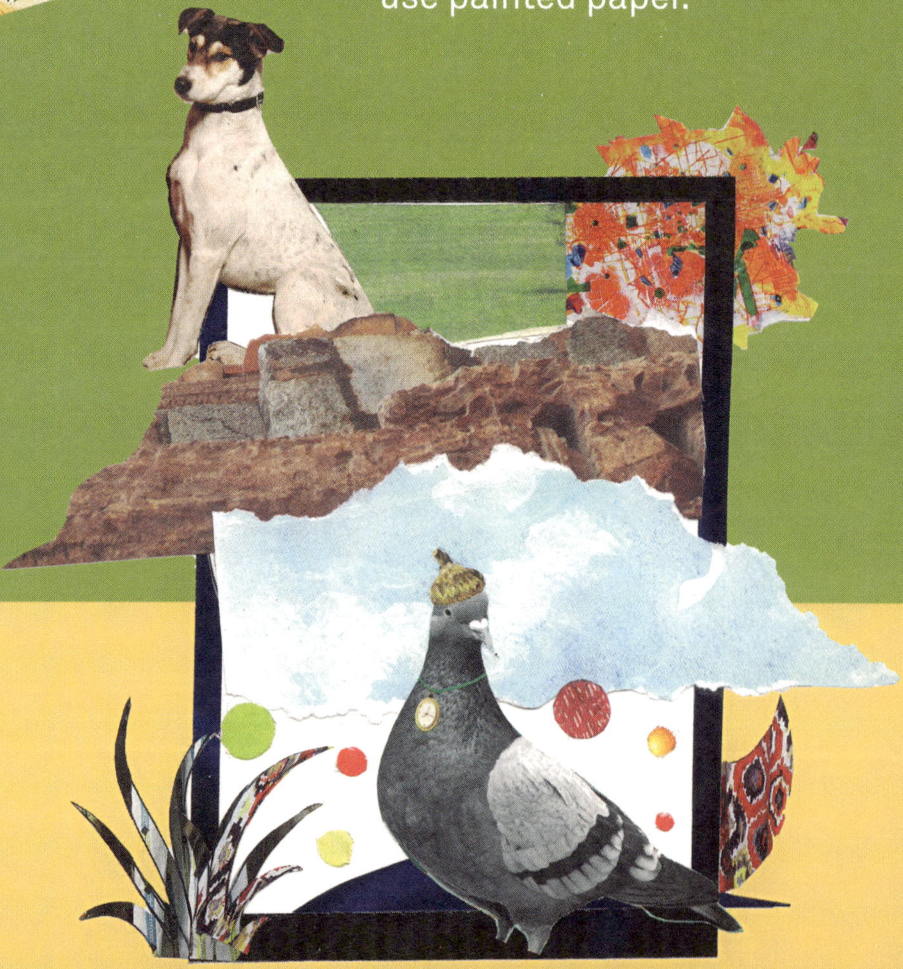

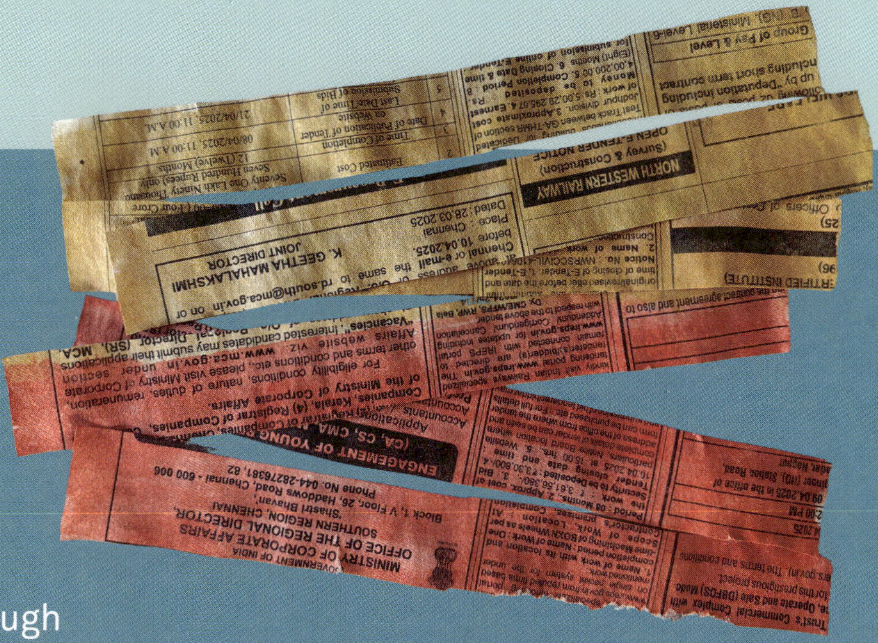

We're going to make a friendly lion with a very special mane.

Let's begin by painting newspapers in shades of browns, oranges and yellows.

You will see the words through the paint, but that's ok—it will add texture to our lion's mane.

Once the painted newspaper is dry, tear it into long strips and set them aside.

You can use shades of orange or brown oil pastel to colour the nose and ears.

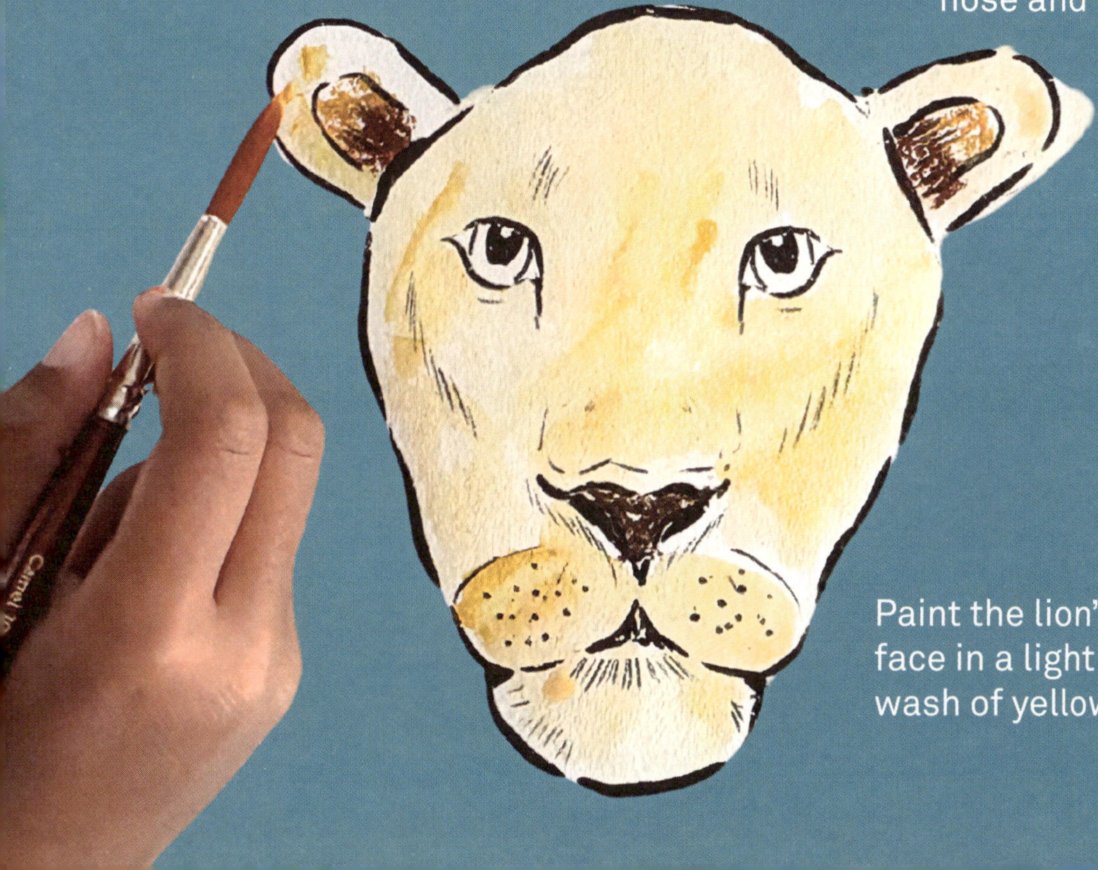

Paint the lion's face in a light wash of yellow.

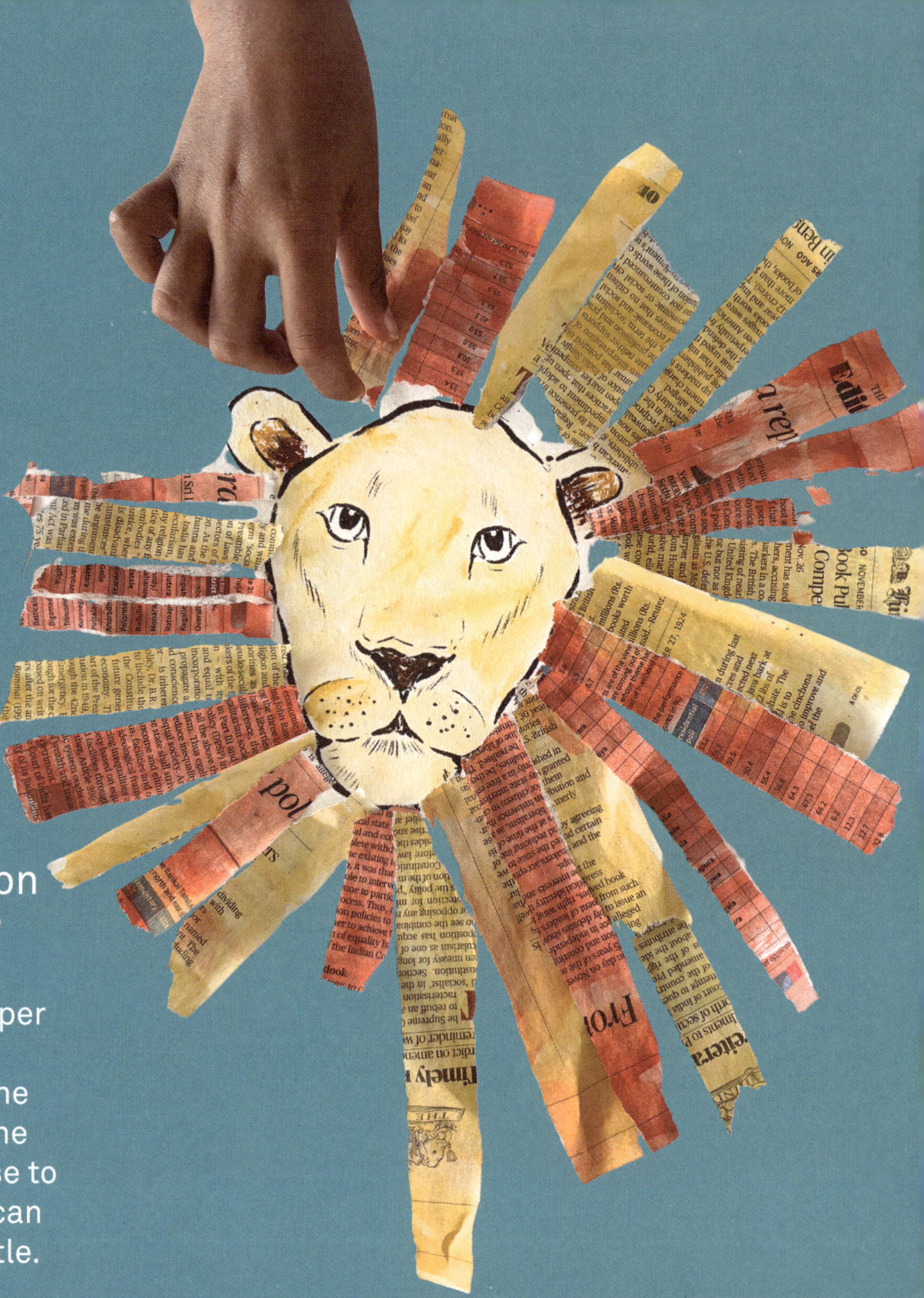

Are you ready to give your lion a furry mane?

Stick the newspaper strips around the lion's face, like the rays of the sun. The strips can be close to each other. They can even overlap a little.

Did you know that lions love to relax? They can sleep for 20 hours a day, to save energy for hunting and other activities. Sounds very relaxing, doesn't it?

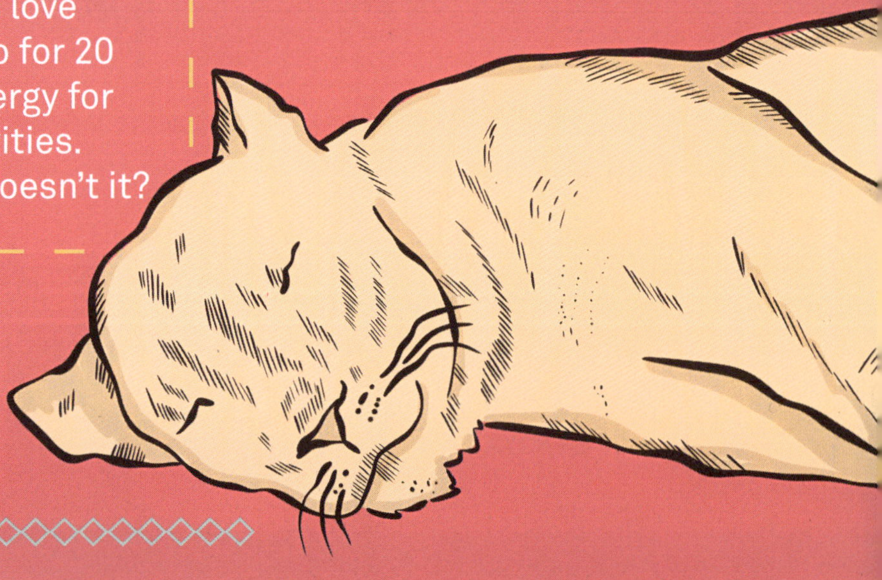

You can have fun painting, tearing and sticking to create your own lion.

ART SUPPLIES: Oil pastels, paints, paintbrush, bowl of water, newspaper, glue

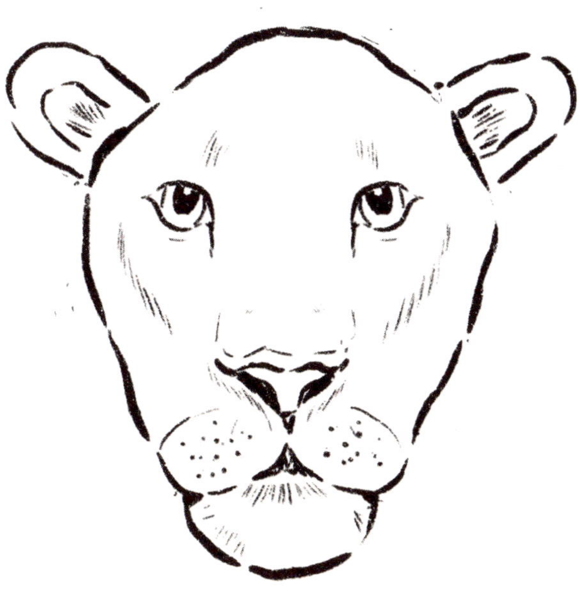

Let's Make a Fun Fish

Are you ready to use everything you learnt to make one last artwork?

Many different types of fish live in oceans, rivers, lakes and ponds. Fish need fins and a tail to help them steer and move faster through the water.

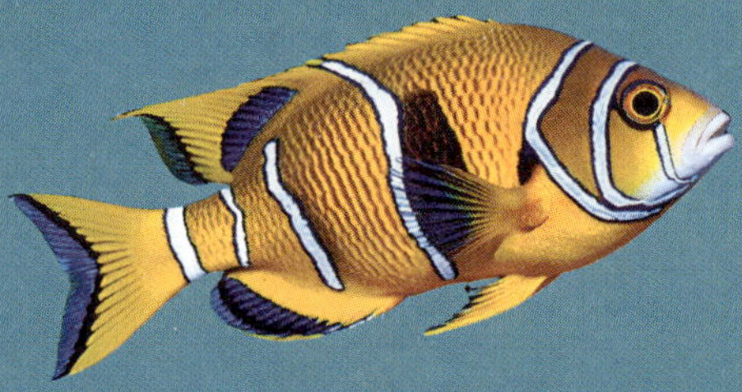

Have you noticed that fish often have colourful patterns?

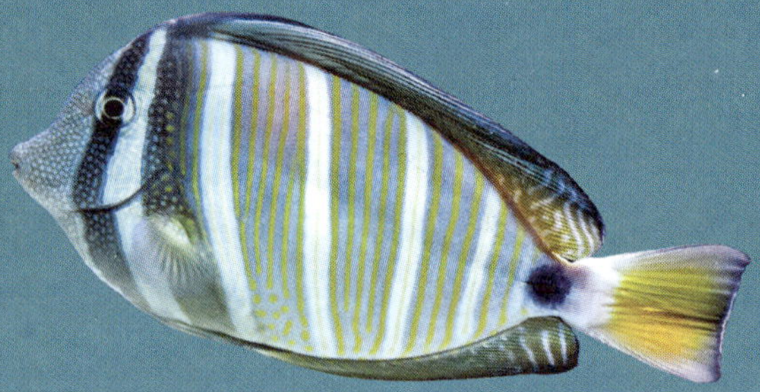

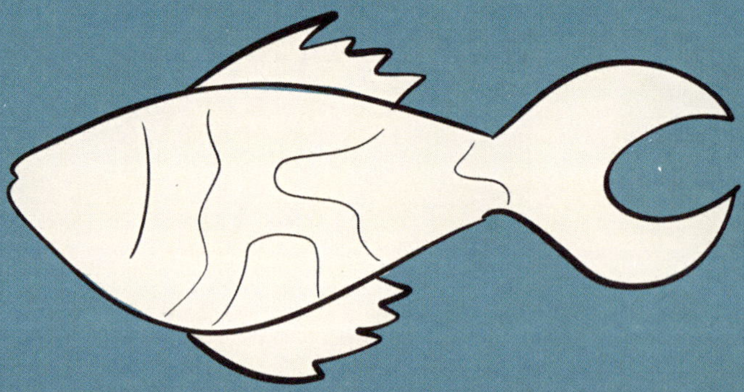

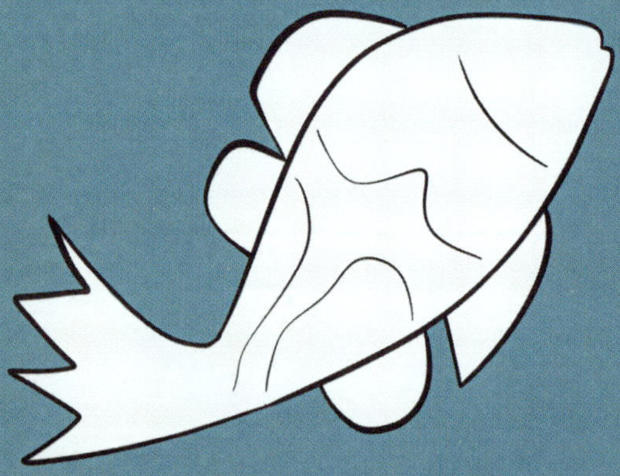

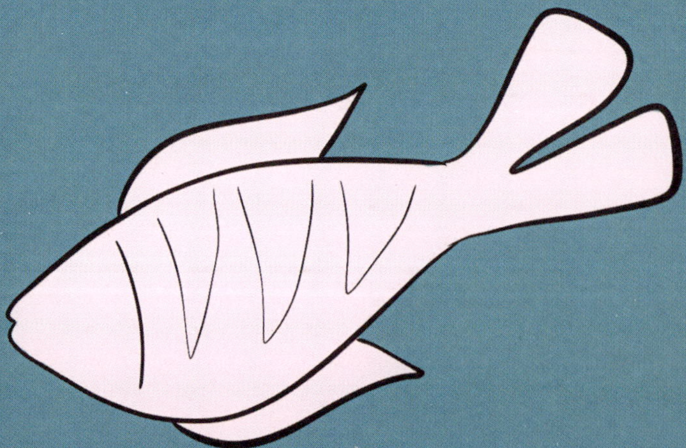

Let's make a fun fish. Use at least two of the new art tricks that you have learnt—oil pastel blending, making patterns or adding fingerprint dots.

Choose bright colours to make intresting patterns on your fish.

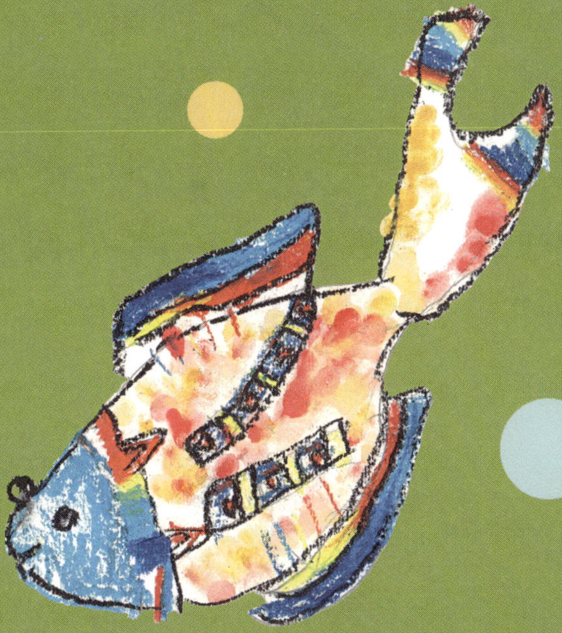

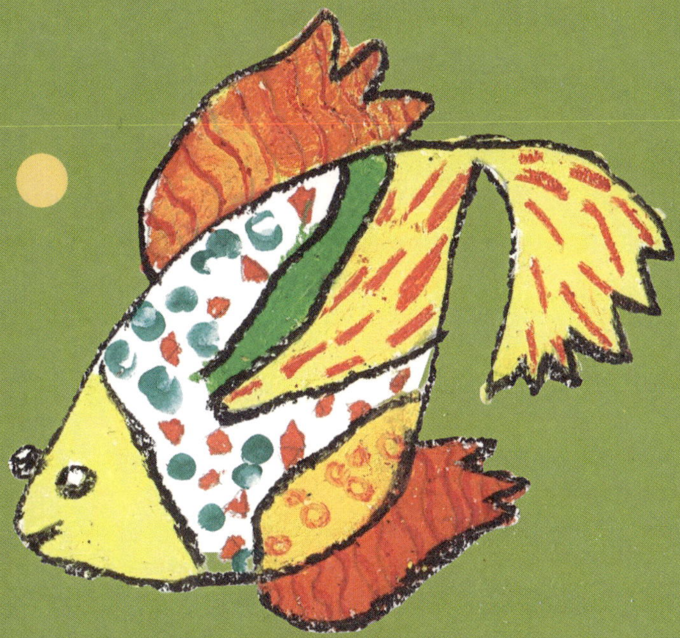

You can use the blending trick—by using two colours to colour the fins and tail.

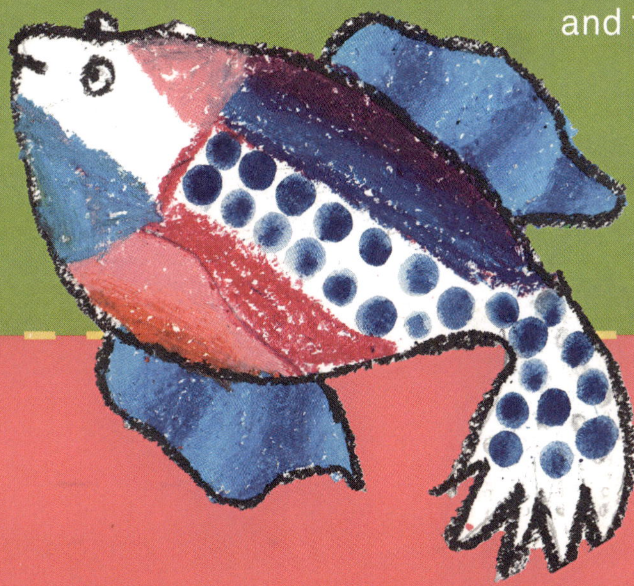

For a final touch, let's use two shades of watercolours to paint the water around your fish. You could use the tissue paper dabbing trick to create the water effect.

Once you're done, paint some newspaper in shades of green, tear it in long strips and stick it around your fish to make seaweed.

Wow! You have learnt many ways to paint and colour.

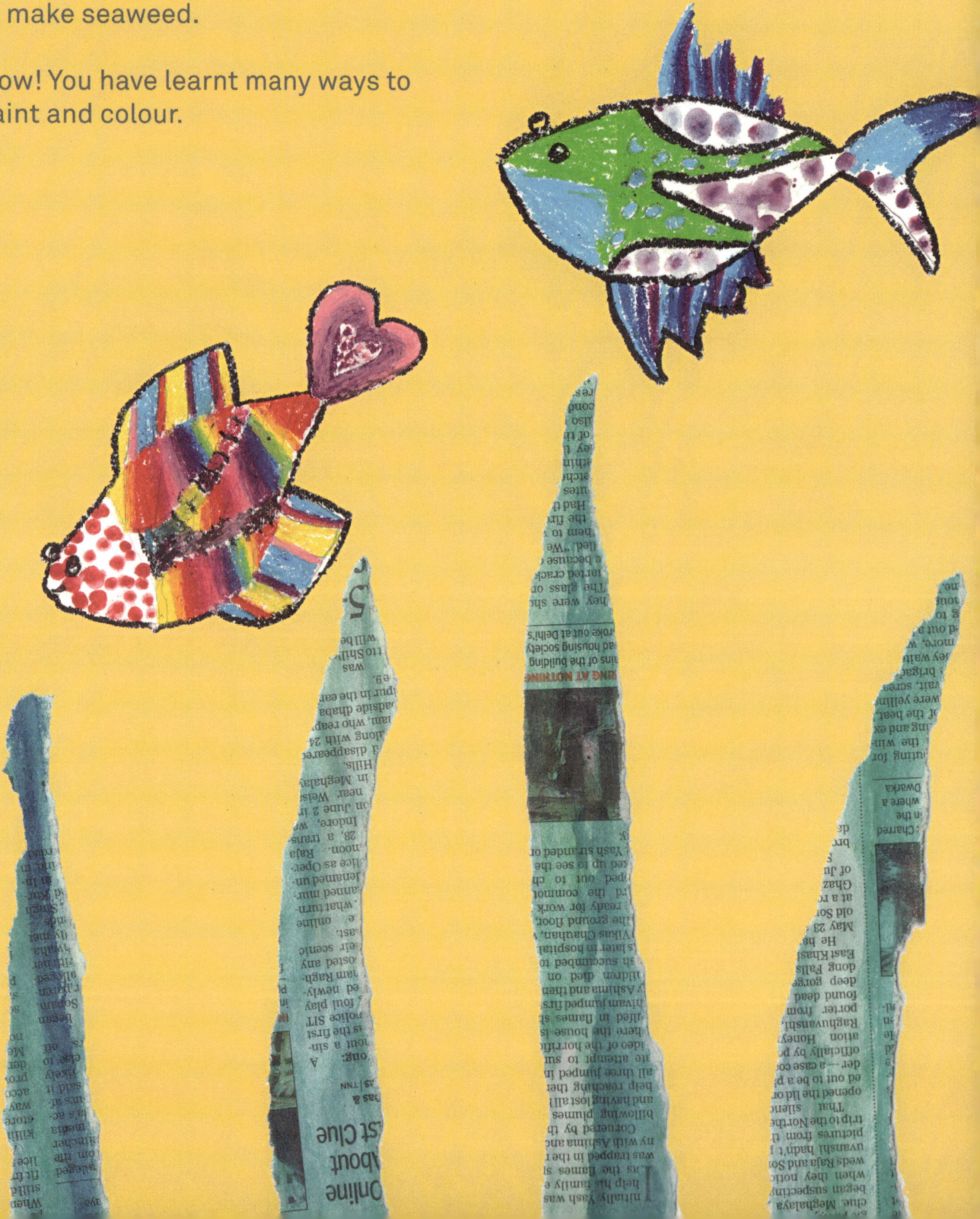

Let's add fins and a tail to this fish. You can use many different ways of colouring and painting each part.

ART SUPPLIES: Oil pastels, paint, bowl of water, paintbrush, newspaper, glue, tissue paper

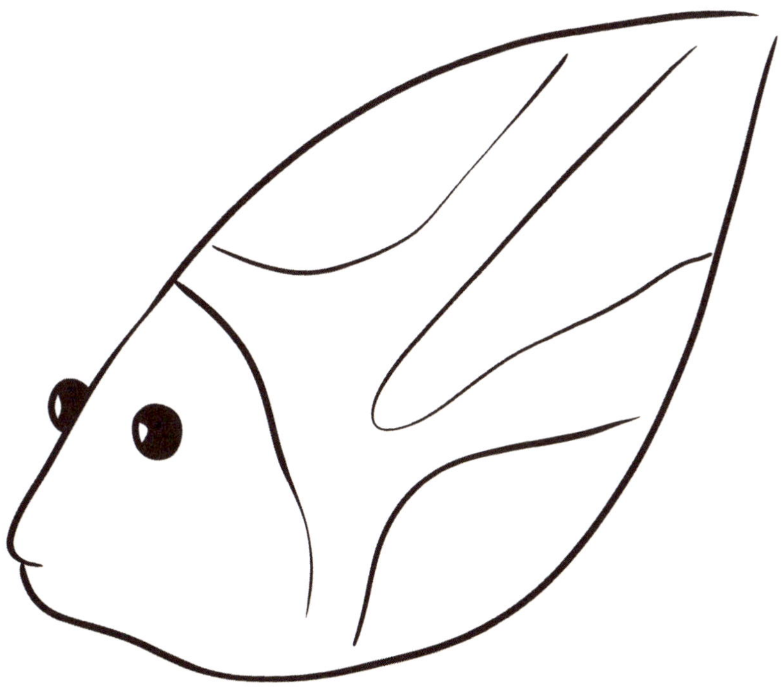

And that's a wrap!

You started with dots and moved on to lines, shapes and textures. You learnt how to outline, make a pattern, blend with two oil pastels and paint with watercolours. You also created different effects using tissue paper dabbing, torn newspaper collage and so much more.

As always, continue to try different things. Have fun, and make art that is as different and special as you are.

Glossary

DOT
A dot is a small round mark. Dots can be used to fill artworks or even make patterns.

LINE
When you make a dot and continue to move your pencil, you make a line.

PATTERN
Repeating the same kind of line, dot or shape many times will make a pattern.

SHAPE
Drawing a line around a space creates a shape. Some common shapes that we know are circle, triangle and rectangle.

TEXTURE
Texture is how something feels when you touch it. Textures can be rough, or smooth, soft or hard.

PRINT
A print is an impression made by painting something that is uneven and then pressing it onto paper.

WARM COLOURS
Warm colours are red, pink, yellow and orange, or any of the colours we see in a fire.

COOL COLOURS
Cool colours are shades of blue, green and purple. Artists often use cool colours to paint plants, the sky or water.

PORTRAIT
A portrait is a drawing, painting or photo of someone's face. It often has their neck and shoulders too. A self-portrait is a portrait made by an artist of their own face.

List of Artworks

Thank you to the many artists, galleries, foundations and museums who gave us the rights to use the beautiful images of artists' works.

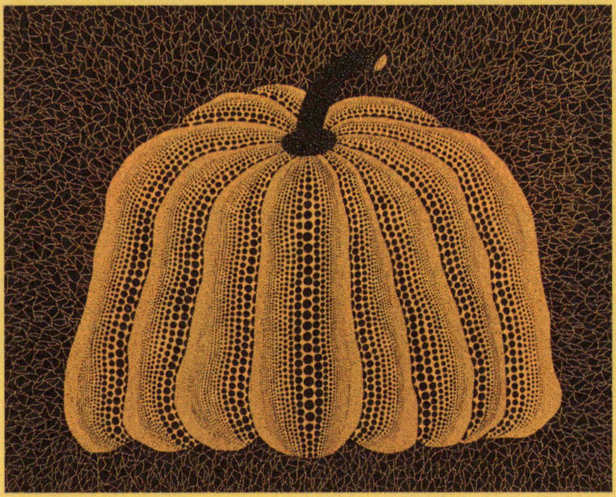

Yayoi Kusama
Pumpkin, 1991
91 x 116.7 cm
Acrylic on canvas

Images facilitated by YAYOI KUSAMA Inc.

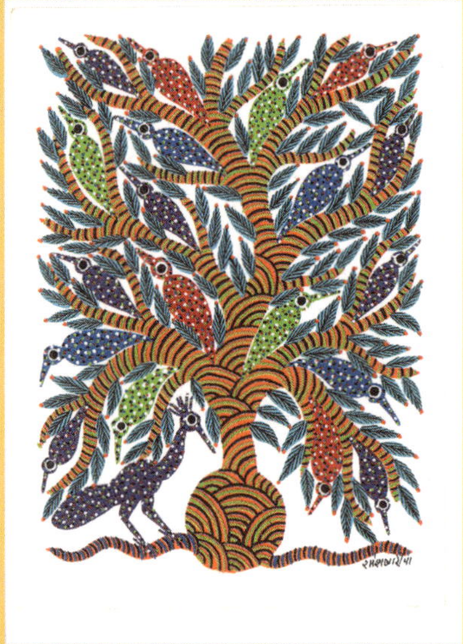

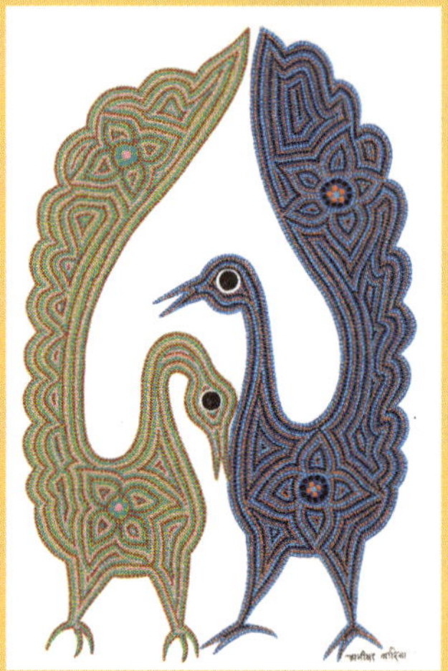

Anisha Bareeya
Jhabua, Madhya Pradesh
Images facilitated by Loksutr

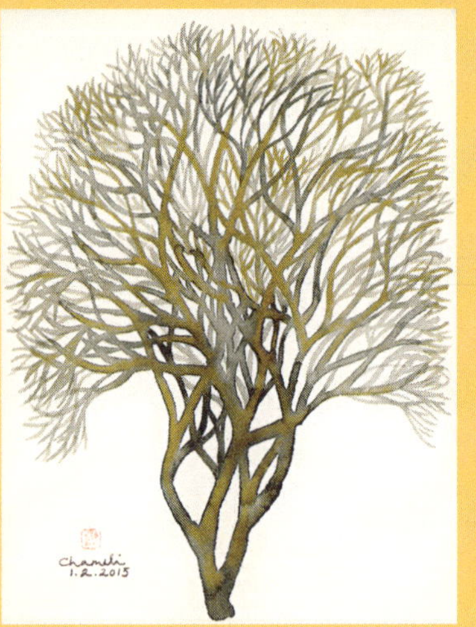

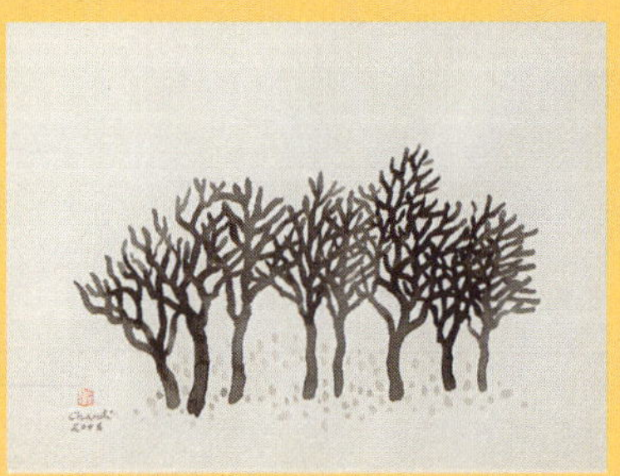

Chameli Ramachandran
Image reproduction rights facilitated by Vadehra Art Gallery

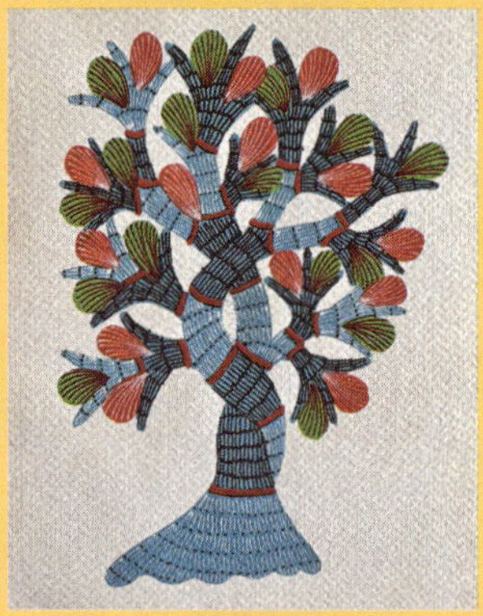

Kailash Kumar Pradhan
Patangarh, Madhya Pradesh
Images facilitated by Loksutr

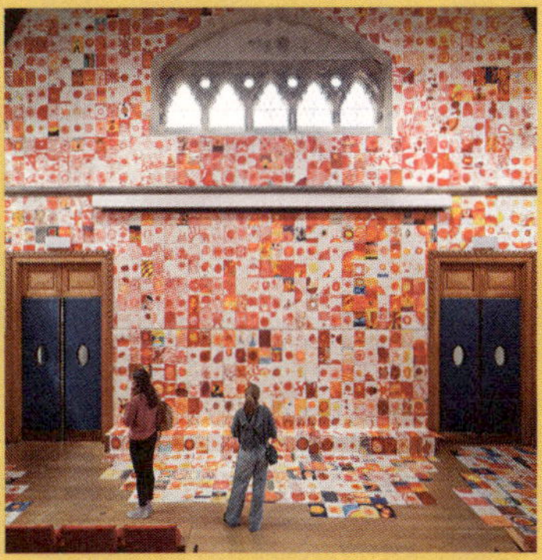

Neil Ghose Balser and Doyel Joshi
Howareyoufeeling.studio
My New Dawn
Commissioned by Brighton Festival, 2025
Guest curator: Anoushka Shankar
Workshop Partner: Amala Aiana

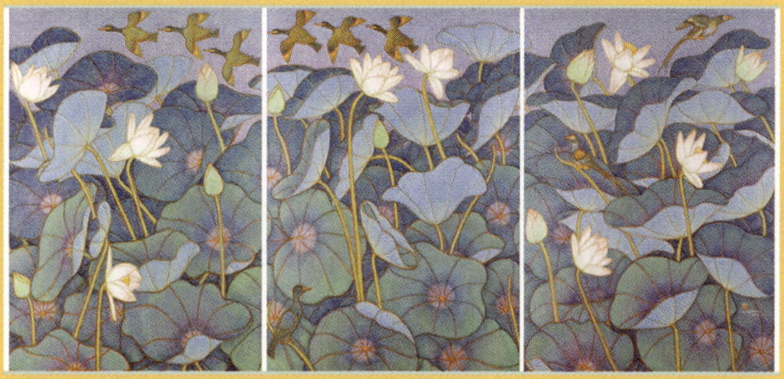

A.Ramachandran
Image reproduction rights facilitated by Vadehra Art Gallery

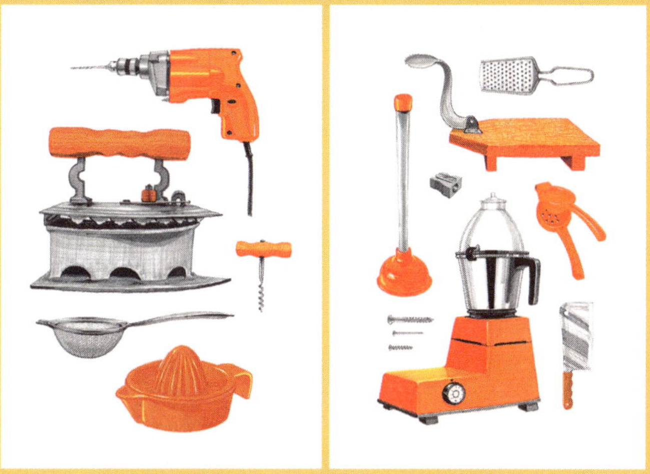

Sameer Kulavoor
City as Objects| Istree
City as Objects| Mixie
Image reproduction rights facilitated by Tarq Gallery

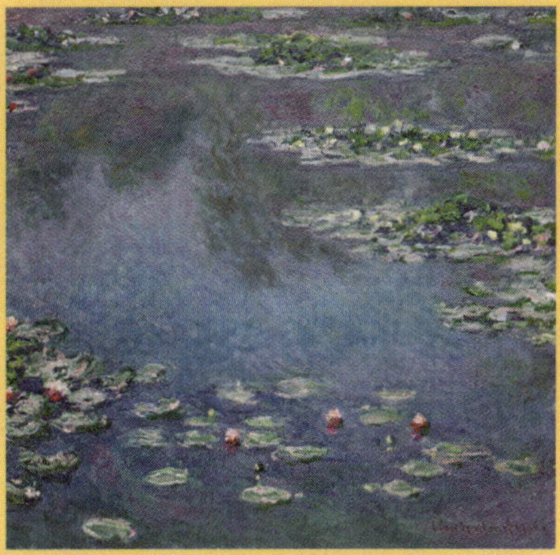

Claude Monet
Water Lillies, 1906
© Mr. and Mrs. Martin A Ryerson Collection
Art Institute Chicago

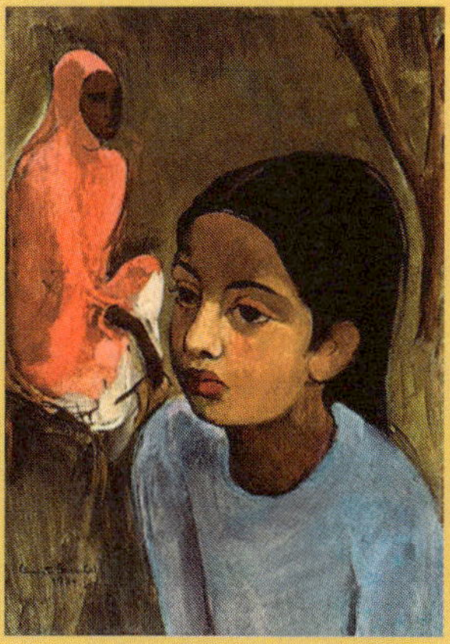

Amrita Sher-Gil
Girl in Blue, 1934
From Amrita Sher-Gil: a self-portrait in letters & writings, introduced, annotated and edited by Vivan Sundaram, volume 1, New Delhi: Tulika Books, 2010, p. 184.
Photo courtesy The Estate of Vivan Sundaram

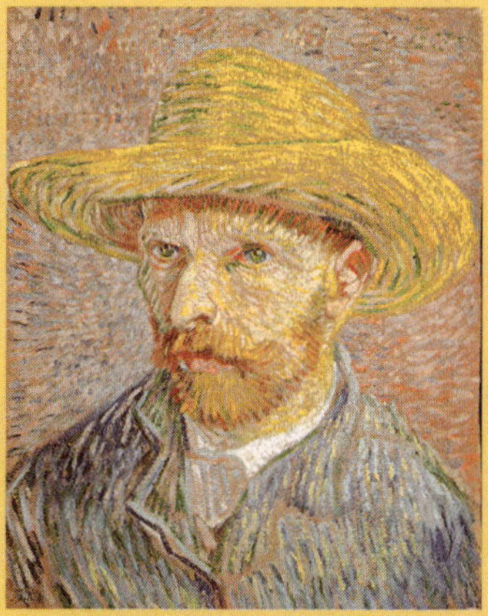

Vincent Van Gogh
Self portrait with a straw hat, 1887
© The Metropolitan Museum of Art, New York

About the Author

Sara is the founder of the RainbowFish Visual Arts program that delivers in-school art lessons to thousands of children in schools across India. She has served as a subject matter expert for NCERT in Delhi and organises conferences and workshops for Art Educators. Sara has also authored several books to introduce children to Indian artists. She completed her graduate studies at Parsons School of Design in New York, where she went on to teach.

You can reach the author at **art@rainbowfishstudio.com**

Acknowledgement

A big thank you to our young artists who tried out our activities with enthusiasm and their parents who kindly allowed us to use their pictures in this book.

Madhava Das | Inara Prakash | Ayra Galada
Armaan Gupta | Sagari Veena Naidu | Devaki Mallika Naidu
Sonali Krishnan | Sonali Shah Genuini